Lucien Stryk is an internationally known poet and translator, the author of fourteen books of poetry, the first of which were produced in England. He has brought out two spoken albums of his work with Folkways Records and is represented in several major anthologies of contemporary poetry.

His translations include *On Love and Barley: Haiku of Basho* and *Triumph of the Sparrow: Zen Poems of Shinkichi Takahashi*. With the late Takashi Ikemoto he translated *Zen Poems of China and Japan: The Crane's Bill* and *The Penguin Book of Zen Poetry*.

He has also published a book of essays, *The Awakened Self: Encounters with Zen*. He is editor of *World of the Buddha: An Introduction to Buddhist Literature* and the anthologies *Heartland: Poets of the Midwest (I and II)*.

Among many awards, he has received the Robert F. Ferguson Memorial Award, the Islands and Continents Translation Award, and, twice, the Society of Midland Authors Poetry Award. He has held fellowships from the National Endowment for the Arts, the National Translation Center, and the Ford and Rockefeller foundations. A former Fulbright scholar and visiting lecturer in Japan, Stryk was a Presidential Research Professor at Northern Illinois University, where he taught poetry and Asian literature until his retirement in 1991.

By the same author

Taproot
The Trespasser
Zen: Poems, Prayers, Sermons, Anecdotes, Interviews
Notes for a Guidebook
Heartland: Poets of the Midwest
World of the Buddha: An Introduction to Buddhist Literature
The Pit and Other Poems
Afterimages: Zen Poems of Shinkichi Takahashi
Twelve Death Poems of the Chinese Zen Masters
Zen Poems of China and Japan: The Crane's Bill
Awakening
Heartland II: Poets of the Midwest
Three Zen Poems
Selected Poems
Haiku of the Japanese Masters
The Duckweed Way: Haiku of Issa
The Penguin Book of Zen Poetry
The Duckpond
Prairie Voices: Poets of Illinois
Zen Poems
Encounter with Zen: Writings on Poetry and Zen
Cherries
Bird of Time: Haiku of Basho
Willows
Collected Poems 1953-1983
Traveler, My Name: Haiku of Basho
On Love and Barley: Haiku of Basho
Triumph of the Sparrow: Zen Poems of Shinkichi Takahashi
Bells of Lombardy
Of Pen and Ink and Paper Scraps
The Dumpling Field: Haiku of Issa
The Gift of Great Poetry
Cage of Fireflies: Modern Japanese Haiku
Zen, Poetry, the Art of Lucien Stryk (edited by Susan Porterfield)
The Awakened Self: Encounters with Zen
Zen Poetry: Let the Spring Breeze Enter

WHERE WE ARE

Selected Poems and Zen Translations

LUCIEN STRYK

With an afterword by
SUSAN PORTERFIELD

SKOOB BOOKS LTD
LONDON

Published in 1997 by

SKOOB BOOKS LTD
11a - 17 Sicilian Avenue
Southampton Row
Holborn
London WC1A 2QH

Design © Mark Lovell

First Edition

ISBN 1 871438 03 9

Printed by WSOY, Finland

British Library Cataloguing-in-Publication Data
A catalogue record for this book is available
from the British Library.

Cover painting: 'Eggplants' by Tsuruzawa Tanzan (1655-1729)
courtesy of the author.

To Helen
again, always

Acknowledgements

This book was compiled with support of fellowships from the National Endowment for the Arts and the Rockefeller Foundation, to both of which I am most grateful. For permission to use poems and essays which first appeared in the following books and periodicals, thanks are due to Swallow Press/Ohio University Press, *Collected Poems 1953-1983* (1984) and *Of Pen and Ink and Paper Scraps* (1989); Northern Illinois University Press, *Bells of Lombardy* (1986), for the poems *In Lombardy* and *Park of the Martyrs*; Penguin Books, *The Penguin Book of Zen Poetry* (1977); Grove/Atlantic, *World of the Buddha: An Introduction to Buddhist literature* (1968) and *Zen Poetry: Let the Spring Breeze Enter* (1975). Poems included in the *Voyage: New Poems* section have appeared in *American Poetry Review, Articulations: Poetry About Illness and the Body*, University of Iowa Press (1994), *1995/1996 Anthology of Magazine Verse & Yearbook of American Poetry, Caprice, Collision, Contemporary American Poetry*, Houghton Mifflin (1996), *Haiku Quarterly, Illinois Review, New Statesman & Society, Partisan Review, Poetry Ireland Review, Printed Matter, Rafters, The Sarajevo Anthology*, Elgin Community College (1993), *Seems, Tamaqua, Willow Review*. The essays included have appeared in *American Poetry Review, London Magazine*, and the *Mississippi Review*.

The Afterword, *Poetry and Lentil Soup*, by Susan Porterfield, first appeared in *Poets and Writers* (1995).

CONTENTS

INTRODUCTION

Several years ago I was invited to contribute an essay on my poetry to a collection. I found the task daunting, yet in searching through criticism for a viewpoint close to my own (thus perhaps authenticating it), I found a passage in T.S. Eliot which struck me as fully suggestive of my own view. It is from an unpublished lecture on English letter writers quoted by F.O. Matthiessen in *The Achievement of T.S. Eliot* and D.H. Lawrence is the subject. Eliot refers to a passage in one of Lawrence's letters, which runs: "The essence of poetry with us in this age of stark and unlovely actualities is a stark directness, without a shadow of a lie, or a shadow of deflection anywhere. Everything can go, but this stark, bare, rocky directness of statement, this alone makes poetry today." And here is Eliot's comment:

> "This speaks to me of that at which I have long aimed, in writing poetry; to write poetry which should be essentially poetry, with nothing poetic about it, poetry standing naked in its bare bones, or poetry so transparent that we should not see the poetry, but that which we are meant to see through the poetry, poetry so transparent that in reading it we are intent on what the poem *points* at, and not on the poetry, this seems to be the thing to try for. To get *beyond poetry*, as Beethoven, in his later works, strove to get *beyond music*."

In the light of such an intense poetic credo it is very moving to read the poet's *Four Quartets*. But I had a comment of my own to make on the Lawrence and Eliot passages:

To get "beyond poetry," then, to avoid the hateful evidence of our will to impress (thereby perhaps losing that ambition), those hand-springs and cartwheels, the heavy breathing down the line, so common to "early work" done at whatever age — the escape from such vulgarity — is the study of a lifetime. . . . A man's poems should reveal the full range of his life and hide nothing except the art behind them.

To illustrate such art I went on to quote, and quote now, my translation of the great Zen poet Shinkichi Takahashi's "Burning Oneself to Death":

That was the best moment of the monk's life.
Firm on a pile of firewood
With nothing more to say, hear, see,
Smoke wrapped him, his folded hands blazed.

There was nothing more to do, the end
Of everything. He remembered, as a cool breeze
treamed through him, that one is always
In the same place, and that there is no time.

Suddenly a whirling mushroom cloud rose
Before his singed eyes, and he was a mass
Of flame. Globes, one after another, rolled out.
The delighted sparrows flew round like fire balls.

Style is the man, one writes what one is. In order to achieve such a poem one has to have extraordinary capacity to *feel*, not necessarily as Zen Buddhist but surely as one able to deal directly with — to return to Lawrence and Eliot — the "stark and unlovely actualities . . . without a shadow of a lie, or a shadow of deflection anywhere." In any age how many can feel so strongly, dare to put as much on the line? It is not only a keen awareness of society that we have every right to expect of our poets, but a probingly severe examination of our spiritual state. Here, translated by George Kay, is Eugenio Montale's "Perhaps One Morning":

Perhaps one morning going along in barren air like glass,
I shall turn around to see the miracle take place:
nothingness at my back, a void stretching
behind me, with a drunk man's terror.

Then as on a screen, assembling themselves in one rush
will come trees, houses, hills, by the accustomed trick.
But it will be too late: and I shall go on quiet
among the men who do not turn, with my secret.

Such poems sustain us, are as essential as bread.

LUCIEN STRYK

PART ONE

The Duckpond

ROOMS

I

The casket under the rose
in the funeral parlor is not
where you live, my mother.

Garbling words for father,
sister, son, aunts, brother-
in-law, wife on an alien

stage, I enter a place high
above daffodils, hyacinths,
tulips of neighboring

gardens, where fire-scaled
butterflies wing free among
leaves, as you sit beside me

in tears at the old kitchen
table, dreading the moment I
leave, a young soldier off to

the Pacific in World War II.
I quietly touch your hand, promise
to take care, write often. In

foxholes, opening mail, I see
you daily, sending your life-line
of words from that room. On

my return, I let myself in to
surprise you sorting my letters
like charms on the bright

checkered cloth. This time
tears come with joy. So what
am I doing making my sermon

here? You are outside the window,
looking in, the monarch you
once made a poem, pure spirit,

wings carrying you above the
rose, to calm your children's,
and their children's, grief.

II

Forward observers, fresh
from mission in the hills
of Okinawa, we crawl back

to our foxholes, under
a battle hymn of mortar
flak and fire, charged

with rumor that our president
has died. Ginger, always
skeptic, rubs his three-day

stubble, mutters —
"At least," "On the contrary,"
"Oh yeah!" Hopsi, the clown,

gulps *Aqua Velva* lotion in
despair. Weary, I lie
in my earth-room, just four

feet deep, rest on my
duffle, feeling the outline
of letters from home, Walt

Whitman's *Leaves of Grass*
under my head. I think
of other times, time that

might never be, cry out
for all the dead. As
howitzers split distance,

and the shells aim back, I
stare up wondering at my
roof of shrapnel and stars.

III

Children's voices strain, round
on round, sweetly breathless,
follow their father, the troubador,

fiddling a chanty in Paris, outside
the church of St. Germain-des-Prés.
The crowd bravos, coins chime on

asphalt. Farther on, a trumpeter
passes his hat in an outdoor café,
where I turn down the street to

the Hôtel de Buci, stop once again
to look into the door. After
thirty-five years, how to explain

to a weary-faced clerk my need
to peer into a room, the size of
a closet, my home for two years

as a GI student back from war.
Trudging there, laden with books,
from the Sorbonne each night, I'd

prop on the sagging bed, back to
one wall, feet up on the other,
stare at the candle's soft flame

in the long dresser mirror. I'd
read through the dictionary, stalking
new words for verse scrawled on

used paper bags, old envelopes
airmailed from home, to the beat
of the asthmatic radiator. How I

would love to climb those stairs once
more, see where it all began. Making
a bold check, in the g's, for granadilla —

where visions of stigmata, nail marks,
thorns became a poem heavy with
may-pops, fruit of the passionflower.

RETURN TO HIROSHIMA

Bombardier

Coming out of the station he expected
To bump into the cripple who had clomped,
Bright pencils trailing, across his dreams

For fifteen years. Before setting out
He was ready to offer both his legs,
His arms, his sleepless eyes. But it seemed

There was no need: it looked a healthy town,
The people gay, the new streets dancing
In the famous light. Even the War Museum

With its photos of the blast, the well-mapped
Rubble, the strips of blackened skin,
Moved one momentarily. After all,

From the window one could watch picnickers
Plying chopsticks as before, the children
bombing carp with rice balls. Finding not

What he had feared, he went home cured at last.
Yet minutes after getting back in bed
A wood leg started clomping, a thousand

Eyes leapt wild, and once again he hurtled
Down a road paved white with flesh. On waking
He knew he had gone too late to the wrong

Town, and that until his own legs numbed
And eyes went dim with age, somewhere
A fire would burn that no slow tears could quench.

Pilot

All right, let them play with it,
Let them feel all hot and righteous,
Permit them the savage joy of

Deploring my inhumanity,
And above all let them bury
Those hundred thousands once again:

I too have counted the corpses,

And say this: if Captain X
Has been martyred by the poets,
Does that mean I have to weep

Over his "moments of madness"?
If he dropped the bomb, and he did,
If I should sympathize, and I do

(I too have counted the corpses),

Has anyone created a plaint
For those who shot from that red sun
Of Nineteen Forty-One? Or

Tried to rouse just one of those
Thousand Jonahs sprawled across
The iron-whale bed of Saipan Bay?

I too have counted the corpses.

And you, Tom Staines, who got it
Huddled in "Sweet Lucy" at my side,
I still count yours, regretting

You did not last to taste the
Exultation of learning that
"Perhaps nine out of ten of us"

(I too have counted the corpses)

Would not end up as fertilizer
For next spring's rice crop. I'm no
Schoolboy, but give me a pencil

And a battlefield, and I'll make you
A formula: take one away
From one, and you've got bloody nothing.

I too have counted the corpses.

Survivors

Of the survivors there was only one
That spoke, but he spoke as if whatever
Life there was hung on his telling all,

And he told all. Of the three who stayed,
Hands gripped like children in a ring, eyes
Floating in the space his wall had filled,

Of the three who stayed on till the end,
One leapt from the only rooftop that
Remained, the second stands gibbering

At a phantom wall, and it's feared the last,
The writer who had taken notes, will
Never write another word. He told all.

THE MINE: YAMAGUCHI

It is not hell one thinks of, however dark,
These look more weary than tormented.
One would expect, down there, a smell more human,
A noise more agonized than that raised
By cars shunted, emptied, brimmed again.

Today, remembering, the black heaps themselves
(On which conveyors drop, chip by chip,
What aeons vised and morselled to lay
A straw of light across the page)
Do not force infernal images.

After weeks of trying to forget,
The eye resists, the vision begged and gotten
Is the heart's: rows of women bent over
Feed-belts circling like blood, pickhammers
Biting at the clods that trundle by,

Raw hands flinging waste through scuttles gaped behind
While, a stone's-throw down the company road,
A smokestack grits the air with substance one
Might sniff below, or anywhere. It marks
The crematory, they pass it twice a day.

CORMORANT

Men speak lightly of frustration,
As if they'd invented it.

As if like the cormorant
Of Gifu, thick leg roped, a ring

Cutting into the neck, they dived
All night to the fish-swelled water

And flapped up with the catch lodged
In the throat, only to have

The fisher yank it out and toss
It gasping on a breathless heap.

Then to dive again, hunger
Churning in the craw, air just

Slipping by the throat-ring
To spray against the lungs.

And once more to be jerked back in
And have the fisher grab the spoil.

Men speak lightly of frustration,
And dim in the lantern light

The cormorant makes out the flash
Of fins and, just beyond,

The streamered boats of tourists
Rocking under *saké* fumes.

ZEN: THE ROCKS OF SESSHU
(JOEI TEMPLE GARDEN, YAMAGUCHI)

I

What do they think of
          Where they lean
Like ponderous heads, the rocks?—

In prankish spring, ducks
          Joggling here
And there, brushing tails,

Like silly thoughts shared,
          Passed from head
To head? When, gong quavering

About a ripened sky, we
          Up and go,
Do they waken from a dream of flesh?

II

In the Three Whites of
          Hokusai —
Fuji, the snow, the crane —

What startles is the black: in
          The outline
Of the mountain, the branch-tips

Piercing the snow, the quills of
          The crane's wing:
Meaning impermanence.

Here, in stainless air, the
          Artist's name
Blazes like a crow.

Distance between the rocks,
        Half the day
In shadow, is the distance

Between man who thinks
        And the man
Who thinks he thinks: wait.

Like a brain, the garden,
        Thinking when
It is thought. Otherwise

A stony jumble, merely that,
        Laid down there
To stud our emptiness.

IV

Who calls her butterfly
        Would elsewhere
Pardon the snake its fangs:

In the stony garden
        Where she flits
Are sides so sharp, merely

To look gives pain. Only
        The tourist,
Kodak aimed and ready for

The blast, ship pointing for the
        Getaway,
Dare raise that parasol.

V

To rid the grass of weed, to get
        The whole root,
Thick, tangled, takes a strong mind

And desire — to make clean, make pure.
        The weed, tough
As the rock it leaps against,

Unless plucked to the last
        Live fiber
Will plunge up through dark again.

The weed also has the desire
        To make clean,
Make pure, there against the rock.

VI

It is joy that lifts those pigeons to
        Stitch the clouds
With circling, light flashing from underwings.

Scorning our crumbs, tossed carefully
        To corners
Of the garden, beyond the rocks,

They rose as if summoned from
        The futile
Groveling our love subjects them to.

Clear the mind! Empty it of all that
        Fixes you,
Makes every act a pecking at the crumb.

VII

Firmness is all: that mountain beyond the
               Garden path,
Watch how against its tawny slope

The candled boughs expire. Follow
               The slope where
Spearheads shake against the clouds

And dizzy the pigeons circling on the wind.
               Then observe
Where no bigger than a cragstone

The climber pulls himself aloft,
               As by the
Very guts: firmness is all.

VIII

Pierced through by birdsong, stone by stone
               The garden
Gathered light. Darkness, hauled by ropes

Of sun, entered roof and bough. Raised from
               The temple
Floor where, stiff since cockcrow,

Blown round like Buddha on the lotus,
               He began
To write. How against that shimmering,

On paper frail as dawn, make poems?
               Firm again,
He waited for the rocks to split.

A PIPE OF OPIUM

When I dropped to the floor
And Jahangir my friend,
Squatting above me, stuffed

The pellets in and lit them,
Enjoining me to puff,
His family started giggling.

At first euphoria of sorts,
Then a quick dissolving: Jahangir
And all his portly brood

Became an undertaker, seven-voiced,
Many fingered, and for an age
I stalked the purgatory

Of his atrocious living room,
Watching the Kerman carpet's
Garden wilt around me,

Feeling the Farsi cackle
Boom against the skull. I rose
Headachy and wiser. There are

Many ways to dodge reality,
Hundreds of states preferable
To the kind of life we own,

But the only satisfactory death
Takes us clean-lunged, clear-headed,
And very much alone.

MOHARRAM
(Islam: month of mourning)

Where we ate in the canyon
The stream reflected, on the crags,
A hundred wavering heads
And the sun falling laced
The water with their blood.
When the sheep grazed down
To clatter round our fire
They wore those heads again,
And the stream had cleansed
The blood from every throat.

Yet none could feel at ease
As, catching our breath, we watched
The shepherd yelp them past
Gorged with the darkened grass.
By that afternoon of Tassua,
Stretched in a great arc of thirst,
The mourners of Hoseyn had flecked
The cragstones with their salt —
Tears, gigantic, rolled down to swell
The trickle misnamed stream.

The water was unfit to drink
And it burned the fingers where
The spits had turned in unbelievers'
Hands. When the sun went down
The sheep, dragging their puffy
Dugs, cropped past again to fold.
Tomorrow was Ashura, day
Of human sacrifice, not sheep's,
And blood would spatter round the gate
Of Imam Reza's Shrine.

Though safely distant, already
We could hear from the city fading
At our backs the cry of "Ya Hoseyn!"
And as on a thousand tambours
Borne as one the rough palms of mourners
Slapped against stripped chests. We bound
The spits, still smelling of our feast,
With wire, and leaving the canyon
To the dark, filed slowly down
The path those jaws had cleared.

THE WOMAN WHO LIVED IN A CRATE

She was very famous: three times she'd sailed
        The world around
In books of photographs, pressed against the
        Imam Reza's Shrine.

Summers she would squat inside the crate,
        Cracked almsbowl up,
Ten *rials* a snapshot, jaw clenched miserably
        For an extra five.

Then as the tourist scuttled off, out poked
        Veiled head, and she
Would crawl onto the sodden road to
        Spit the money clean

And gossip with the roadsweep's mule. Guiltily
        We bore her scraps
Until we saw it was ourselves, trapped in
        Thick-walled crate, we might

Have pitied: no-one picked shamed way through
        Steaming mule-turds
To fill a leaky almsbowl, while we sat
        Tittering in the sun.

18

OBJET D'ART

The copper bowl I keep
       Tobacco
In is thick with nightingales

And roses, up to the
       Minaret
Its lid, incised so-so.

I no longer smoke in
       Company,
It seems indecent:

Reminded by those birds
       And flowers
Of a botched renown,

A Persian I once
       Had for tea
Turned from it and wept.

A SHEAF FOR CHICAGO

Something queer and terrifying about Chicago:
one of the strange "centres" of the earth . . .
- D.H. *Lawrence to Harriet Monroe*

I. Proem

Always when we speak of you, we call you
Human. You are not. Nor are you any
Of the things we say: queer, terrifying.

It is the tightness of the mind that would
Confine you. No more strange than Paris
Is gay, you exist by your own laws,

Which to the millions that call you theirs,
Suffice, serve the old gargantuan needs.
Heaped as if just risen — streaming, unsmirched —

From seethings far below, you accept all.
By land, air, sea they come, certain to find
You home. For those you've once possessed, there's no

Escaping: always revealed in small
Particulars — a bar, a corner — you
Reappear complete. Even as I address

You, seeing your vastness in alleyways
And lots that fester Woodlawn, I have
A sense of islands all around, made one

By sea — that feeds and spoils yet is a thing
Apart. You are that sea. And home: have
Stamped me yours for keeps, will claim me when,

Last chances spent, I wrap it up for good.
You are three million things, and each is true.
But always home. More so and more deeply

Than the sum of antheaps we have made of
You, reenter every night to dream you
Something stone can never be. And met

However far away, two that call you
Home, feel beyond the reach of words to tell
Like brothers who must never part again.

II. A Child in the City

In a vacant lot behind a body shop
I rooted for your heart, O city,
The truth that was a hambone in your slop.

Your revelations came as thick as bees,
With stings as smarting, wings as loud,
And I recall those towering summer days

We gathered fenders, axles, blasted hoods
To build Cockaigne and Never-never Land,
Then beat for dragons in the oily weeds.

That cindered lot and twisted auto mound,
That realm to be defended with the blood,
Became, as New Year swung around,

A scene of holocaust, where pile on pile
Of Christmas trees would char the heavens
And robe us demon-wild and genie-tall

To swirl the hell of 63rd Place,
Our curses whirring by your roofs,
Our hooves a-clatter on your face.

III. The Balloon
(To Auguste Piccard, his day at Soldier Field)

As you readied the balloon, tugging
At the ropes, I grabbed my father's hand.
Around us in stone tiers the others

Began to hold their breath. I watched my
Father mostly, thinking him very
Brave for toying with his pipe. Then when

You filled the giant sack with heated
Air and, waving, climbed into the
Gondola with a bunch of roses

Thrust at you, I freed my hand, cheered
And started clapping. I caught your eye,
You smiled, then left the ground. The people

Filed for exits when, twisting in
The wind, you veered above the lake, a
Pin against a thundercloud. But I

Refused to budge. My father stooped to
Beat me and cracked his precious briar
On the stone. And still I wouldn't leave.

He called me a young fool and dragged me,
Bawling, to the streetcar. But I couldn't
Stop watching you. I stayed up all that night,

Soaring ever higher on your star,
Through tunneled clouds and air so blue
I saw blue spots for hours. In the morning

My father laughed and said you came back down.
I didn't believe him then, and never will.
I told him I was glad he broke his pipe.

IV. The Beach

Even the lake repulses:
I watch them where, shellacked
       And steaming

In barbaric light, they
Huddle in their shame, the maids
    And busboys.

Even the lovers dare not
Step where the goddess rose in
    Tinted foam,

But paw each other, gape,
Spin radio dials. And hulking
    Over cards

Mothers whip strings of
Curse like lariats, jerking
    The children

From the shore when, suddenly
Across the beach, they hear:
    "Lost! Child lost!"

None rise. The breakers drown
Voices, radios; peak white, pound
    In like fists.

V. Mestrovic's Indians
(Equestrian statues, Michigan Avenue)

With bare heels sharp as spurs
They kick the bronze flanks of
    The horses.

But what sane beast would brave
A river wild as this, choked
    As it is

With jagged tin and all
That snarling rubber? And
    Ford to where?

Along the other bank, while the
Great arms pointing with their
        Manes convulse

In anger, the merchants
Dangle strings of gewgaws
        In the sun.

But no mere hoof was meant
For plunging here, and why, the
        Horses seem

To ask, would even redskins
Climb a shore where not one
        Grassblade springs?

            VI. City of the Wind

All night long the lake-blast
        Rattled bones of
Dreamers in that place of glass.

Awake, they heard a roaring
        Down the lots and
Alleyways where wind flung

Rainspout, fencepost, toolshed,
        As if the town
Were tossing on the flood

Of space. All night, it seemed,
        A horde of giants
Came trampling overhead,

Tore limbs, wrenched screens, spilled
        Glass like chips of
Sky. Next day through, the dazed

Ones rooted in the mire,
        Then, back in beds,
Dreamt the city fairer

Than before. But how,
        Snapped antennae
Pulling roofs askew,

Autos tipped hub-deep in silt,
        Could dream raise up
What dream alone had built?

VII. Eve

In Calcutta I found her in a stall,
        A thing for sale,
Breasts like burnished gourds: some things one does
        not buy.

In Isfahan her eyes were black as wells
        Entreating alms
Of all who passed: there are deserving charities.

In Amsterdam above a darkened street
        A bay window
Framed her sundries, proffering bliss: I was not sold.

In Seville she wore a gypsy shawl and
        Bangles on her
Dancing feet: the silver dropped around them was not
        mine.

In Paris she hugged me down the avenue,
        Skirt a jocund
Sail, towed by the dollars in my purse: I tacked for
        home.

In Chicago she waits behind a door
        No common key
Can budge: who enters there will never get away.

VIII. The Gang

One can hardly extricate them
From the props they lounge against,
Or see them for the smoke lips

Link in chains that will not hold.
At night the sound of pennies tossed
Upon the sidewalk-cracks is like

A slowly breaking mirror
Which reflects the little that they
Are. What girl dare pass and not

Be whistled at? Their appraisements
Are quick, absolute: that water
Freezes into ice needs scant

Deliberation. Whatever
The day sweeps up, their sole
Antagonist is boredom, which

By merely standing around, they
Thwart at every turn but one.
They scorn whom others envy,

The man who ambles by, duty
Snapping at the heels, and should lovers
Cross, there is a sudden flinging down

(By eyes so starved, they almost moan)
And then a coupling in the dust.
Allow them such years to lean

And wait. Soon they must approach
The selfsame corner, and hail
The gang that is no longer there.

IX. The Neighborhood

Long away, I find it pure
Exotic; no matter that they roll
The sidewalks up at ten and boys

Want height to leap for basketballs:
It is a place, and there are corners
Where one does what one would do.

Come back, I find the expected
Changes: shabby streets grown shabbier,
The mob all scattered, old girl friends

Losing more of what's been lost,
The supermarts turned up like sows
To give the brood of grunters suck,

And Mother, like a thickening tree
Whose roots work deeper as the woodsman
Nears, spread over all, the wind which sweeps

Across her whispering "Stay on."
Two weeks of that, and there are
Other whispers that I heed.

The train pulls in and I descend,
To mount before it pulls away.
Goodby Mother, goodby! I'm off

Again to Someplace Else, where
Chafing together once a month
The strangers sit and write sweet letters home.

SNOWS

I

All night thick flakes have fallen,
The street below lies smothered
    With the past.
One remembers other snows
    (Images
In snapshots framed by the chill
Edge), ablaze before the thaw.

II

Disburdenment is what mind seeks
Above all other riches,
    Disburdenment
Of little griefs gathered like drifts
Into each corner. I think of
    This as, shovel
Arcing wide, breath peopling the air,
I hurl slosh like diamonds at
    A snout of sun.

CHEKHOV IN NICE

I

Along the Boulevard des Anglais
Tourists mistook him for Lautrec,
Though he was taller
And when not hunched over hacking
His walk was straight enough.

Perhaps it was the way he stared
At women, like a beggar
At a banquet window, and then
He was always scrabbling for a notebook
While the snickering revelers

Flowed like water round a stone.
Oh they all knew him artist.
All, that is, except the people
He would talk to in his
Scant atrocious French: the waiter,

The cabdriver, the man who
Brought his boots back in the morning
Like an oblation to Apollo.
To them he was a munificent
White Russian, title snatched,

A parcel of serfs languishing
For his return. Certainly
He was unhappy. And the chambermaids
Were touched by nailmarks
Through the blood-flecks on his sheet.

The century had just turned over,
And the Côte was never gayer.
Even the dowagers, strapped
To beachchairs all along the shore,
Felt young again and very beautiful.

And rather scornful, he was quick
To see, of the old-young man
Who moved among them like a noctambule,
His back to Mother Russia,
Seagulls screaming at his ears.

II

He had just turned forty, and now
At times he felt himself regretting.
Oh they had expected far too much
Of one as sick and poor, hung with
Unmarried sisters and a widowed dam.

Wasn't it enough to have planted
The usual imaginary garden?
Must he also, like some poet,
Sing upon the ruddy boughs?
Were he less the son, he'd have come

Here twenty years ago. Before those
Germs, swarming, had carved
A kingdom of his chest, before
The flame had risen from his bowels
To fan within his head. Were he less the son . . .

And the reputation, so harshly won,
Did precious little good in France.
Who'd risk displeasing one who'd make of her,
However high her beauty,
A thing of pity in some dismal tale?

Foutu! he muttered as he slunk
Back to his room and tossed his hat
Upon the pile of doodled papers
On the desk. Now he longed for home.
In the few years left to him

Would come — was bound to come —
Another thirty stories and a dozen plays.
Then no doubt they'd prop his bones
Between those giants in Novo-Devechy.
But were there any choice to make, he'd act

The part of one the world was still applauding,
That country squire of his,
Petulant, bored, pining for the Côte d'Azur,
And — if one could believe those Russian hacks —
Likely to live forever.

NOTES FOR A GUIDEBOOK

In celestial Padua
The ghosts walk hugely
In the public squares.

Donatello is one,
His horseman in the
Piazza San Antonio
Guards the gruff saint's heart
Like a mystic ruby,
The ears of the horse,
Of the rider,
Riddled by prayer.

Giotto, Dante are others,
The painter's frescoes
Float like clouds
Above the city,
The poet's cantos
Ring upon its walls.

And what of us,
Who stand with heads
Strained back, feet tapping?
Shall we eat, sleep,
Be men again?
Shall we slip back

To the whores of Venice? —
Dwarfs, clods, motes of dust
In the brightness.

31

THE FOUNTAIN OF AMMANATI
(Piazza della Signoria, Florence)

Below the pigeon-spotted seagod
The mermen pinch the mermaids,
And you shopgirls eat your food.

No sneak-vialed aphrodisiac
Can do — for me, for you — what
Mermen pinching mermaids in a whack

Of sunlit water can. And do.
These water-eaten shoulders and these thighs
Shall glisten though your gills go blue.

These bones will never clatter in the breath.
My dears, before your dust swirls either up
Or down — confess: this world is richly wet.

And consider: there is a plashless world
Outside this stream-bright square
Where girls like you lie curled

And languishing for love like mine.
And you were such as they
Until ten sputtering jets began

To run their ticklish waters down your
Spine. Munch on, my loves, you are but
Sun-bleached maidens in a world too poor

To tap the heart-wells that would flow,
And flow. You are true signorine
Of that square where none can go

And then return. Where dusty mermen
Parch across a strand of sails and spars,
And dream of foamy thighs that churn.

AT VIRGIL'S TOMB

The bus stops just outside the gate
    Where all day long
The kids retrieve their soccer ball.

I watch and wait (in Ravenna
    Your Florentine
Lay starred on every tourist's map,

And gendarmes' pikes, like gladioli,
    Blazed around him).
Now as the tour-bus honks below

I imagine another Beatrice
    Entreating you,
In glory's dream, to guide her lover

Through that flaming labyrinth.
    At last you speak:
"Tell him to live remembering you,

Say that long ago man's boot ground through
    Inferno's crust,
The world he made, and will not know."

SNIPER

An inch to the left
and I'd be twenty years
of dust by now. I can't

walk under trees without
his muzzle tracks me.
He'd hit through branches,

leaves pinned to his shoulders
whistling. We searched him
everywhere — up trunks,

in caves, down pits. Then
one night, his island taken,
he stepped from jungle

shade, leaves still pinned
upon him glistening
in the projector's light,

and tiptoed round to watch
our show, a weary kid
strayed in from trick-or-treat.

STEVE CRAWLEY

Why whenever they mention Hawaii
Do I think of you, and not the hula
Girls or orchids shrill against the blue?
Why when they send postcards of tourists tense
Around a burning pig, leis like collars
On a brace of hounds, do I see you flung
Across the earthfloor of that tent again,
Brains like macaroni puddled at the ear?

Steve Crawley, we found her letter crushed
Between the oilcan and the rosary
On your cot, and thought we understood,
But what puzzles still is this: what were you
Doing in that cathouse line, all brass
And itch, the night before the letter came?

THE PIT

Twenty years. I still remember
The sun-blown stench, and the pit
At least two hundred yards from
The cove we'd anchored guns in.
They were blasting at the mountains,
The beach was nearly ours.

The smell kept leaking back.
I thought of garbage cans
Behind chopsuey restaurants
Of home, strangely appealing on
A summer's night, meaning another
Kind of life. Which made the difference.

When the three of us, youngest in
The crew, were handed poles and told
To get the deadmen underground
Or join them, we saw it a sullen
Sort of lark. And lashed to trees,
The snipers had us dancing.

Ducks for those vultures in the boughs,
Poles poking through the powder-
Bitten grass, we zigzagged
Toward the pit as into
The arse of death, the wittiest
Of us said but did not laugh.

At last we reached it, half full
Of sand and crawling. We clamped
Nose, mouth, wrenched netted helmets
To the chin, yet poles probed forward
Surgically, touching for spots
The maggots had not jelled.

Somehow we got the deadmen under,
Along with empty lobster tins,
Bottles, gear and ammo. Somehow
We plugged the pit and slipped back
To the guns. Then for days
We had to helmet bathe downwind.

I stuck my pole, clean end high,
Behind the foxhole, a kind of
Towelpeg and a something more.
I'd stare it out through jungle haze,
And wonder. Ask anyone who
Saw it: nobody won that war.

SPEECH TO THE SHAPERS

They are wrong who think the end will be
Violent, rank alarmists who have
Visions of bombs bursting east and west
Together, leaving their hillocks of

Dead. Or who sniff already in the
Wind the poisons that will circle and
Devour. They have not lived enough who
See great armies joined along a strand

By nothing more than the bayonets
They'd stabbed into each other's innards,
With, to complete the savage picture,
Vultures and, moored with flesh, the buzzards.

And what must one really think of those
Who leap from Bibles reciting Doom,
When not only every Doom so far
Recited has failed, like rain, to come

But even the callowest Sunday
Schooler grins? The end will steal upon
Us as an average day, sometime between
Breakfast and lunch, while Father is down

At the office, Junior playing ball
And Mother is choosing lambchops at
The butcher's. Unannounced, it will drop
From a cloudless sky, or like a cut

In the power take us by surprise,
With all the lights snuffed out together.
But far more than the lights will go out,
And whatever's wrong will not appear

To be wrong, and it will have begun not
The day before, or now, or even
A thousand years ago. There's the rub.
We'll never know what hit us where, or when.

THE FACE

Weekly at the start
of the documentary
on World War II

a boy's face, doomed,
sharply beautiful,
floats in the screen,

a dark balloon
above a field of barbs,
the stench of gas.

Whoever holds the
string
will not let go.

LETTER TO JEAN-PAUL BAUDOT, AT CHRISTMAS

Friend, on this sunny day, snow sparkling
everywhere, I think of you once more,
how many years ago, a child Resistance

fighter trapped by Nazis in a cave
with fifteen others, left to die, you became
a cannibal. Saved by Americans,

the taste of a dead comrade's flesh foul
in your mouth, you fell onto the snow
of the Haute Savoie and gorged to purge yourself,

somehow to start again. Each winter since
you were reminded, vomiting for days.
Each winter since you told me at the Mabillon,

I see you on the first snow of the year
spreadeagled, face buried in that stench.
I write once more, Jean-Paul, though you don't

answer, because I must: today men do far worse.
Yours in hope of peace, for all of us,
before the coming of another snow.

AWAKENING
Homage to Hakuin, Zen Master, 1685-1768

I

Shoichi brushed the black
on thick.
His circle held a poem
like buds
above a flowering bowl.

Since the moment of my
pointing,
this bowl, an "earth device,"
holds
nothing but the dawn.

II

A freeze last night, the window's
laced ice flowers, a meadow drifting
from the glacier's side. I think of Hakuin:

"Freezing in an icefield, stretched
thousands of miles in all directions,
I was alone, transparent, and could not move."

Legs cramped, mind pointing
like a torch, I cannot see beyond
the frost, out nor in. And do not move.

III

I balance the round stone
    in my palm,
turn it full circle,

39

slowly, in the late sun,
    spring to now.
Severe compression,

like a troubled head,
    stings my hand.
It falls. A small dust rises.

IV

Beyond the sycamore
dark air moves
westward —

smoke, cloud, something
wanting a name.
Across the window,

my gathered breath,
I trace
a simple word.

V

My daughter gathers shells
where thirty years before
I'd turned them over, marveling.

I take them from her,
make, at her command,
the universe. Hands clasped,

marking the limits of
a world, we watch till sundown
planets whirling in the sand.

VI

Softness everywhere,
snow a smear,
air a gray sack.

Time. Place. Thing.
Felt between
skin and bone, flesh.

VII

I write in the dark again,
rather by dusk-light,
and what I love about

this hour is the way the trees
are taken, one by one,
into the great wash of darkness.

At this hour I am always happy,
ready to be taken myself,
fully aware.

RITES OF PASSAGE

Indian river swollen brown and swift:
the pebble from my hand sounds above
      the southfield —

soybeans, corn, cicadas. Stone rings
touch the bank, ripple up my arm.
      In the grass

a worm twists in webbed air (how things
absorb each other) — on a branch
      a sparrow

tenses, gray. As grass stirs it bursts
from leaves, devouring. I close my book.
      With so much

doing everywhere, words swimming green,
why read? I see and taste silence.
      Starlings flit,

blue/black feathers raising spume
of dandelions, young fluttering
      in the twigs.

I think of my grown son who runs
and heaves me to my feet — our
      promised walk

through woods. As he pulls back a branch
hair on his forearm glistens
      like the leaves

we brush by. I follow down the path
we've loved for years. We try to
      lose ourselves,

yet there's the river, churning south.
I muse on what I've given,
        all I can't.

My son moves toward the bank, then turns.
I stop myself from grasping
        at his hand.

SOUTH

Walking at night, I always return to
        the spot beyond
the cannery and cornfields where

a farmhouse faces south among tall trees.
        I dream a life
there for myself, everything happening

in an upper room: reading in sunlight,
        talk, over wine,
with a friend, long midnight poems swept

with stars and a moon. And nothing
        being savaged,
anywhere. Having my fill of that life,

I imagine a path leading south
        through corn and wheat,
to the Gulf of Mexico! I walk

each night in practice for that walk.

THE GOOSE

Magnificent
against October maples
the goose
twisting in downdraft
shot to the highway,
crushed on my wheels —
I braked
wanting to rush out,
imagined
its strong arc south again.

Blaring cars
shadowed
as I started up,
driving for miles
in innocence
in guilt
not caring where I headed,
a whiteness
mangled
in the maples, everywhere.

FARMER

Seasons waiting the miracle,
dawn after dawn framing
the landscape in his eyes:

bound tight as wheat, packed
hard as dirt. Made shrewd
by soil and weather, through

the channel of his bones
shift ways of animals,
their matings twist his dreams.

While night-fields quicken,
shadows slanting right, then left
across the moonlit furrows,

he shelters in the farmhouse
merged with trees, a skin of wood,
as much the earth's as his.

THE QUAKE

Alone in that paper house
We laughed when the bed
Heaved twice then threw
Us to the floor. When all

Was calm again, you said
It took an earthquake
To untwine us. Then I
Stopped your shaking

With my mouth. Together
In this place of brick,
Held firm as fruits
Upon a sculptured bough,

Our loving is more safe.
Then why should dream
Return us to that fragile
Shelf of land? And why,

Our bodies twined upon
This couch of stone,
Should we be listening,
Like dead sinners, for the quake?

DREAMING TO MUSIC

Windstorm thrums
the window, drizzles
the maple's flame.

So begins another
summer's end. As I
turn up the stereo

a girl in Rheims
walks out of a medieval
love song, lifts

her brocaded gown
along the mucky path
out of the woods,

shortcutting through
a wheatfield silvered
in cloudburst, toward

the farmhouse gate.
Flicking the latch she
looks back, whispers

her passion to the rain,
this Sunday afternoon,
six centuries late.

HYDE PARK SUNDAY

Suddenly the bronzed Spaniard,
yellow bandanna on his forehead,
left his companions with a leap —
perfect somersault — then cartwheeled
past the lovers on the grass.

The sprawlers gaped, on Speakers' Corner
there was silence, those angry men
turned blessed, forgiving —
so much pure energy expended for nothing,
for absolutely nothing.

ELEGY FOR A LONG-HAIRED STUDENT

He called at four a.m.: about to fly
to Mao, he had to know the Chinese word
for peace. Next day he was dead.

"Such dreams were bound for madness,"
I told his mourners. "He was too good
for this world." "He would have wanted you,"

they said. "*You* understood." Bearing
his body to the grave, I saw the long red hair
he could not stop from coiling round

their throats: Elks, Legionnaires.
Unmocked now, it would grow. As we lay
him down, I spoke that word for peace.

THE LOCUSTS

Whirring from the desert, so dense
      We thought the sand
Was heaving to engulf us,

The locusts raised a wind. Sunlight
      Scarcely filtered
Through, then, sudden decimator,

The car made paste-and-membrane
      Of their swarming,
Trophied where a hundred spanning

Wings and wrenched sky-hopping legs
      Had clung. We moved
Through famished miles, blind, remembered

Plagues as thick and foul about us.
      Reaching town, I
Hosed the car down for a day,

Then sold it. Today whenever
      I think of her,
Locusts, locusts, break around me.

BOSTON

South Station, very early, and
come to read midwestern poems
at Tufts, due in an hour, seedy

in my all-night-slept-in suit,
I need a shave. The john of Savarin's
is full. I try the public one.

A bum is scraping skin off
at the mirror. I stand behind him,
fumble for the switch, lift

my cordless shaver to the jaw.
The tattooed stripper on his arm
begins to bump. Soap drips bloody

from his straightedge. "Give it here,"
he mutters. Razor plowing down,
I know he means it, hand

it to him, juice full on,
grab my suitcase, then half shaved
move off to read those poems.

THE EXCHANGE

As I turned from the bar,
my back to him,
he beat it through the door
with every cent I had.

"Happens everyday," the barkeep
said. I burned for weeks,
imagined trapping him
in alleyways, fists ready.

Then his face lost focus,
I found myself remembering
the tip he gave me
on a horse, his winning manner

and his guts. I'd learned
at some expense
a truth about myself,
and was twice robbed.

AMPUTEE

Something kept the blood from
going round —
he gave up one leg like a prize,

and then the other. Soon it would
be his arms.
He called it an "unwilling heart."

Jollying nurses, once he rocked
the ward with —
"Who's for football?" from his bedpan throne.

When he was readied for the saw again,
we wished him
well. He waved his bandaged hand:

"Now you see it, now you don't,"
he quipped. They
told us he died laughing under gas.

BUSKER

Facing the playhouse queue,
straining through songs

all can remember, she muffs
a high note at the end.

As we start to shuffle in,
she scrambles for the loot.

Fat, seedy — never mind —
she is so purely what she is

no actor could do more.
Leaving the queue, I follow

her all night, hands full of coins,
songs ringing everywhere.

MUSEUM GUARDS (LONDON)

I

He smokes against the wall
blowing rings where Moore's giants
escape through the holes

in themselves. He is small among
them, and his cigarette, the one
live thing, fizzles in the rain.

II

You would have understood what made
the guard leap from his chair
and, pointing at your saints,

cry out in Italian —
"What am I doing here?" Carlo Crivelli,
what is wrong with this world?

III

He watches us watching, weary,
cough straightening his slouch.
Seven years facing the Watteaus.

Life's no picnic. Ask him, the crippled
one who used to whisper shyly
that he was an artist, waiting for the break.

MEMO TO THE BUILDER

. . . and then
After the roof goes up
Remember to lay the eave trough
Wide and deep. A run
For squirrels and a river
For my birds. You know, I'd rather

You made the trough
So, than have the rooftop
Tarred and shingled. Keep
It in mind, the trough.
Also I'm not so sure of glass
In every window. But let that pass.

Still — and there are
Reasons enough, believe me —
It would please no end to be
In and out together.
And how it would thrill me should a bird,
Learning our secret, make a whir —

ring thoroughfare
Of a room or two.
Forget the weather. To
Have the wild, the rare
Not only happen, mind, but
Be the normal is exactly what

I'm after. Now
You know. Perhaps you
Think I've made your job too
Light? Good. Throw
Caution to the beams. Build me a home
The living day can enter, not a tomb.

FISHING WITH MY DAUGHTER IN MILLER'S MEADOW

You follow, dress held high above
    the fresh manure,
missing your doll, scolding Miller's horses

for being no gentlemen where they graze
    in morning sun.
You want the river, quick, I promised you back there,

and all those fish. I point to trees where
    water rides low
banks, slopping over in the spring,

and pull you from barbed wire protecting corn
    the size of you
and gaining fast on me. To get you in the meadow

I hold the wire high, spanning a hand across
    your freckled back.
At last we make the river, skimmed with flies,

you help me scoop for bait. I give you time
    to run away,
then drop the hook. It's fish I think

I'm after, you I almost catch, in up to knees,
    sipping minnowy
water. Well, I hadn't hoped for more.

Going back, you heap the creel with phlox and marigolds.

THE DUCKPOND

I

Crocus, daffodil:
    already the pond's
        clear of ice

where, winter long,
    ducks and gulls
        slid for crusts.

People circle —
    pale, bronchitic,
        jostling behind dogs,

grope toward lawnchairs
    spread like islands
        on the grass.

Sunk there, they lift faces to the sun.

II

Good Friday.
    Ducks carry on,
        a day like any other.

Same old story:
    no one seems to care.
        A loudmouth

leader of a mangy host
    spiked to a cross,
        as blackbirds in certain

lands neighboring on
    that history are splayed
        on fences, warning

to their kind. A duck soars from the reeds.

III

Man and woman
    argue past the duckpond,
        his arms flaying,

she, head down — even
    by the fully budded
        cherry, clustered

lilac boughs. Not once
    do they forget
        their bitterness,

face the gift of morning
    ducks wake to
        in the reeds.

They have things to settle, and they will.

IV

On my favorite
    bench beside the roses
        I watch ducks

smoothing feathers,
    breathing it all in.
        Catching the headline

where the bird flits
    I'm reminded
        three men were shot up

at the moon. I turn
    back to the roses:
        what

if they don't make it? If they do?

V

Lying near the pond
    in fear of the stray
        dog that daily

roams the park,
    ducks know
        their limitations,

and the world's —
    how long it takes,
        precisely,

to escape the paw thrusts
    of the dog,
        who once again

swings round to chase his tail.

VI

Radio tower
    beyond the blossoms,
        ducks

here in the pond,
    a connection
        between them —

how did I discover
    this, and why?
        Was it

the blue air? The bench
    moves beneath
        us like a seesaw,

the pond sends news of the world.

VII

What becomes of things
    we make or do?
        The Japanese lantern

or from across the pond
    beneath the trees
        a drift

of voices cultured
    and remote: water
        will carry anything

that floats. The lantern
    maker, the couple
        chatting there

would be amazed to find themselves a poem.

VIII

When tail wagging
    in the breeze
        the duck pokes

bill into the pondbed,
    keeps it there,
        my daughter thinks

him fun — he is, yet how to say
    those acrobatics
        aren't meant

to jollify the day. He's
    hungry, poking
        away at nothing

for crumbs we failed to bring: how to tell her?

IX

Ducks lie close together
    in morning dew, wary-eyed,
        bills pointing at the pond:

roused by squirrels,
    those early risers,
        air's a-whir with wings.

Sad to think of leaving
    this place. A helicopter
        with mysterious purpose

appears above the trees,
    moving low. Its circles
        tightening,

the ducks cling to the pondedge, right to fear.

PART TWO

Willows

WHERE WE ARE

I sit beneath the linden's
heart-spread leaves, watch

three starlings on the bird-
bath watching me. Book on

one knee, I drain my glass:
young shoots, already doomed,

thrust withering tendrils
through the clay-bogged soil.

Last night, at the May Fair,
girls in Elizabethan garb

offered a madrigal to buds
of spring. Today the neighbor's

cat stalks fledglings in the
pine. Time was I'd run him

off. Now I just sit and trust
to his bad luck. Slowly sun

tinges leaves, hazes pine
needles. A mower sputters —

cat leaps from the shade,
into the moment, where we are.

CHERRIES

Because I sit eating cherries
which I did not pick
a girl goes bad under

the elevator tracks, will
never be whole again.
Because I want the full bag,

grasping, twenty-five children
cry for food. Gorging,
I've none to offer. I want

to care, I mean to, but not
yet, a dozen cherries
rattling at the bottom of my bag.

One by one I lift them to
my mouth, slowly break
their skin — twelve nations

bleed. Because I love, because
I need cherries, I
cannot help them. My happiness,

bought cheap, must last forever.

SCRAP PAPER

I'm strapped into the oral
surgeon's bogey-chair. The scene
of Northern woods upon the wall

swirls into years of pipe smoke
as the needle hits the dark
vein of my hand, sends me groping

over mounds of textbook
galley sheets, generously donated
by a friend. The brambled

type threads business jargon
through my images, whips pines,
percentiles, graphs into one puff.

So much for more than thirty years
of fine-cut Latakia, sweet
Virginia. As finger-printed carbons

fill my lesioned roof of mouth,
I choke off dark, somehow to
find a clearing where I stumble on

the arms of wife and son, back to
a woozy world of masks made up
of pen and ink and paper scraps.

NOVEMBER

First frost, the blue spruce
against my window's shagged,
and the sky is sombering. I

draw close to the fire, inward
with all that breathes. This
morning, stacking firewood,

I shattered leaf-drifts by
the shed, trailing the rabbit
burrowed there. Soon we'll

be wintering, he and I, our
paths will often cross upon
the snow. I drink good

luck to both of us, he in his
sticks and leaves, and I in
mine. Summer, the neighbor

blamed his marauding for the
shrinking salad patch, hinting
the yards would be well rid

of something two dogs, even
a tent of wire could not keep
out. I muttered to myself,

dropped my carrot like a
calling card behind the shed.
Now the spruce twists slowly

into dark. I pour another
drink. Within the hour the moon
will kindle every frosted limb.

ELM

Beetles smaller than
rice-grains hollowed
the weathered trunk,

piling sawdust high.
Fearing another storm
might axe the sparse-

leafed branches through
the shingles, I loosed
bird-feeder ropes, gave

up the elm to Shabbona
Tree Service. Watched
birds spiral, squirrels

bolt as limbs crashed
down. By afternoon, sun
warmed the jagged stump,

and the stone-roof once
overhung with leaves. Season
turning, frost spiked

the twigless air. Soon
snow filled emptiness
between the shrubs. I

fed my elm-logs to the
fire, sending ghost-
blossoms to the sky.

OLD FOLKS HOME

Always near dusk
in the shadow of
cedars, he mourns
the loss of another

day. The empty path
winds to fields pulsing
gold, green under
vapors, rain-fresh

furrows stretching
miles. Each afternoon
the old man ambles
under branches,

remembering his farm,
wife long dead, sons
buried in lives
of their own. There

he stands hours, keen
to the cool scent
of fullness — now
without purpose where

corn-tassles blow.
Returns to the bare
room, high above cedars,
gathering gold and green.

CALENDAR

Another year: curbs
strewn with Christmas
trees, tinsel floats

the thaw. We've stumbled
to the end, driven by
storms still rumbling

overhead. Earth speaks
what we already know,
in pain relearn. On

the wall the Japanese
calendar, pure of our
devisings, mists beyond

peaks, temples, pines
where we survive. Page
by page guards secrets,

as we start out again.

ÉTUDE

I was cycling by the river, back and forth,
    Umbrella up against the
        Rain and blossoms.

It was very quiet, I thought of Woolworth
    Globes you shake up snowstorms in.
        Washed light slanted

Through the cherry trees, and in a flimsy house
    Some youngster practised Chopin.
        I was moving

With the current, wheels squishing as the music
    Rose into the trees, then stopped,
        And from the house

Came someone wearing too much powder, raincape
    Orchid in the light. Middle-aged,
        The sort you pass

In hundreds everyday and scarcely notice,
    The Chopin she had sent
        Up to those boughs,

Petals spinning free, gave her grace no waters
    Would reflect, but I might
        Long remember.

WATCHING WAR MOVIES

Always the same: watching
World War II movies on TV,
landing barges bursting onto

islands, my skin crawls —
heat, dust — the scorpion
bites again. How I deceived

myself. Certain my role would
not make me killer, my unarmed
body called down fire from

scarred hills. As life took
life, blood coursed into
one stream. I knew one day,

the madness stopped, I'd make
my pilgrimage to temples,
gardens, serene masters of

a Way which pain was bonding.
Atoms fuse, a mushroom cloud,
the movie ends. But I still

stumble under camouflage, near
books of tranquil Buddhas by the
screen. The war goes on and on.

SIBERIA

Small wood towns silvered
    by birches,
sharp blue at windows, doors.

Grimed, forgotten domes,
    a gold cross:
cows, chickens haunt the tombs.

Train lurches on: ten miles west
    of Irkutsk,
where Chekhov, bound for convict

Sakhalin, once spent the night,
    I hear three
sisters longing, Moscow, Moscow!

At the Siberian heart, concrete
    crammed with facts:
who produced what, how much, when,

in what spirit. On the
    last ruled sheet
a finger-smudge points like

a holy candle. November: in
    seven days
drums, bugles, flags will whip

town after town. On wind-
    scourged platforms
throngs mill under likenesses

of hero farmers — ribboned,
    bemedaled,
exalted by a fourth sister,

one Chekhov did not know, who
        pitying
her sisters' discontent accepted

solitude and hardship, despite
        the need, at
times unbearable, of Moscow, Moscow!

CHRIST OF PERSHING SQUARE

"I can prove it!" the madman cried
And clutched my wrist. "Feel where the nails
Went in! By God, I bear them still!"

Half amused, I shrugged and let him
Press the hand against his suture:
"All right," I said, "they cut you up."

Suddenly those fingers grasped
A hammer, it was I had hoisted
The cross his flung arms formed there.

"Yet," I whispered, "there remains
The final proof — forgiveness."
He spat into my face and fled.

This happened in Los Angeles
Six months ago. I see him still,
White blood streaming, risen from

Cancerous sheets to walk a Kingdom.

YOU MUST CHANGE YOUR LIFE

Of all things one might be:
a squirrel lopes by

busy at being himself
in a tough nutless world,

cats at his young, rain
slanting in his nest,

night falling, winter
not provided for —

no questions to ask
of himself or anyone.

IN OUR TIME

When after the blast
they turned to the poet,
he asked for a handful
of nails. Pounded them
like phrases into old
boards. No bittersweet,
no roses now. He knelt
in silence in the wasted
town — a stain under the
fallout moon. Nails, line
by line, his only song.

SAVANTS

Their hour had come
and gone: notions
blueprinted, years

of infinite zeros,
halved, quartered,
atomed for this day —

test-tubes of dust
measured to shake the
world. Now it was

done. Reaming traces
from their nails,
scattering like rocks

they'd blasted from
the earth, they turned
to raking gardens,

lecturing on peace,
regrets black-signatured
across an ashen page.

Secret codes unlearnt,
they crawled back to the
past on hands and knees.

SALVATOR ROSA (1615 - 73)

Strong sun on the Tuscan
town where he painted
did not flush the somber

face of his revolutionist
(that head meant for axing)
propped on the easel, rough

hands unrolling a banner
with — goosequilled in
haste — "Silence, unless

what you have to say
is better than silence."
As sunlight entangled the

hills inquisitors ranted,
rebellion was whispered in
shade. Rosa worked on, deepening

eyes of his saints, risking
slogans on canvas. And
that was better than silence.

IN LOMBARDY

So near Verona: eye centers
beyond peaks silhouetted
in the distance, turns back

centuries to Pisanello, taking
time out from medallions to
paint his *Vision of St. Eustace*,

my thirty year rapture at the
National Gallery, London. Here,
in the clear frame of the sky,

I see Christ crucified across
the antlers of a stag, while
creatures of the earth, this

luminous hour, forage at peace
in rich grass. Today, creators
of bold theories on the mind would

see hallucination where the
artist stroked all suffering in
his saint, who waits, hand raised

before his chest, poised at the
trembling edge, sensing the world's
glinting arrow speeding toward

the stag's, and his own, heart.

PARK OF THE MARTYRS OF LIBERTY

Downhill, I pass snails opaling the way,
saunter by waterfalls of miniature
snapdragon. Entering the square of

San Giacomo, I am confronted by a name
on the old convent wall: Teresio Olivelli,
patriot, tortured, murdered in Hersbruk Camp,

aged 29. Restless, I question friends,
officials, strangers — who shrug, as if
so much reality could only blight a poem.

I stalk for traces, ferret out of silence
a poet-professor, officer of the famed
Alpine unit routed on the Russian front,

who, given up for lost, outflanked a blizzard,
two wounded comrades in his arms: bemedaled
National hero, recovering by this shore,

illusions fizzled in clear light on water.
He joined, reorganized the freedom-
fighters. Betrayed, imprisoned, twice escaped,

betrayed again, comforting fellow inmates
to the last. His "Prayer of the Rebel" lived
on. "We were rebels for love," he said.

Going back up through the public garden,
I pause where German tourists picnic,
lean against a rock bearing three names:

Teresio Olivelli, partisan, killed by Nazis,
                              17.1.45;
Tino Gandola, partisan, shot down in the street,
                        aged 18, 9.7.44;
Ninetto Gilardoni, partisan, slain in savage
                    combat at Vallsolda, 29.11.44.

The tourists' children climb the rock,
bombard their fathers with blood-red azalea
petals, as guidebooks in hand, day-trippers

shadow footprints of Liszt and his lady,
unaware this garden is a shrine to greater
love. I rest upon a bench nearby, recalling

Saipan, Okinawa, fallen friends. More
than an hour I sit here —
watching the blind go by, in martyrs' park.

WIND CHIME

Wind stirs a bonfire of
October maples. I take off
with my daughter, son, his

wife and son, for woods on
Indian river. Years we've
trespassed through this maze

of creatures, sharing wild
grapes, walnuts, mushroom
puffs. Tangling with hail-fellow

mosquitoes. Tracked through
snowdrifts, storms, up to this
stand of poplars, listening

to wind-chime icicles. Today
as autumn shreds and patches up,
we hear the strumming leaves,

watch branches weaving light
into the clouds, know each time
we return might be the last.

CROW

He is made giddy by the sun,
And is stupid enough to race
Its rise and fall, so that at dawn

One spots him lumbering across the
Winter sky, then perched like a heart
Within the skeletal tree.

Wherever he goes he carries
His stomach like a weapon,
And the small bird hungering flies

In his wake, hoping for a crumb
As the foul beak chews and caws
Together and the black wings climb.

Devourer of acres, he drops
On the puny scarecrow and plants
Tomorrow's morsel between the flaps

Of its straw-stuck coat. Nothing
Frightens him, the hawk will whirl
From what he swoops for, this king

Of field and fat metropolis.
And already taken over
From the eagle, he must replace

That ancient master of the sky
On escutcheon and dollar.
In this usurpation he

Most resembles us: image of
Our gutty need and power, he
Merits all our rubbish and our love.

BOTANIST
(Sweden, 1986)

The season leaning into
winter in Uppsala, my friend
    Lennart and I

warm up with coffee in
a second-floor cafe. Look
    out the window

at the year-end remnants
of Linnaeus' Garden, speak
    of the harmony

of rows, the rage for order.
Remembering the Latin cry
    for Clarity, I

see now what I lack, wonder
why this handsome young
    translator of plays

and poems chose to take on
a voice lost in wild and
    unnamed grasses where

birds, so namelessly alive,
return from unknown regions every
    spring, to swoop

where gold untitled flowers
light leaf-fossils through
    old winter's mud.

FISHING WITH CASPER
(Sweden, 1986)

Ringed by shadow-heads of pines
we drift over Stromaren, Lake of Storms,
in bright nippy air, trailing

Old Pike, the one who never fails
to get away. Casper gives
the rod to me, hoping for stranger's

luck, rows us from point to point
where, he says, fish abound. As
the line grows heavy I pull in my catch,

a clump of tangled reeds. Through
the swift-darkening afternoon, forest
closing in, my friend consoles me,

certain there will be no fish-fry
back in Orbyhus tonight, where his wife
and children wait us in their sprawling

house inside the castle grounds. There,
over schnapps, sharp herring, moose,
crisp tart snowberries we laugh together,

chat of icefishing and poems, canny pike
and bass, still warmed by light-arrows
piercing water, a moment of October sun.

CONFESSION

When with my stuffed beginner's hook
      lodged in his lip
the small-mouth bass shot up
and almost ditched the rowboat, I jerked
      the flyrod high.

Caught there, eye to eye, we flashed
      together in
the sun, flyrod ablaze
between us — midspace, midlife —
      then the plunging.

I dream him down there still,
      crawdad sucked to
bone, flyrod clicking on the lakebed
where, shrunk from the anchored hulls,
      he slowly spins.

SOUTHERN TALE

From deep in the town the dancers' stomp
Will not rouse him now,
Where he hangs like a cracked bell:
Dark engulfs the man, the ashen cross.

The girl steps back and dreams —
O he the night and she the slippery moon,
And high the cotton flew!
It was like swimming in the river,
Water pressing to her deeps,
Ropes the arms that pulled her down,
The river banging on the wharf.

She looks away, her whiteness
Blending with the moon,
And hears the flies
Maddened by the smell of horse,
The smell of flesh.

From deep in the town the dancers' stomp
Will not rouse him now:
The arms, tongue,
Giant thighs are mute.

LAMENT FOR WELDON KEES

Could we have known that torrid night
A book of yours would sell
For eighteen dollars, we might

Have gotten a little drunker.
Weldon, where the blazes are you?
I can't help thinking of your

Wife, the lovely way she
Had of listening, holding her
Pride in you like a virginity.

We talked of poems, your "Robinson,"
And then you shuffled back
To slap some more paint down,

The canvas flat upon the table,
Under a light so fierce I thought
The paint would run. You didn't call

It that, but painting was your hackwork,
And surely the hope of poet's ease
Held you there from dark to dark,

The gin beside you on a stool.
I was green as grass, and you
My first live poet. What a bloody fool

You must have thought me! But it
Wasn't your praise I wanted then,
And thank Christ you knew that.

Just to be with you, and talk,
And drink your gin was what I'd
Come for. I left your room to walk

The city ragged, knowing at last
That poets were quite human.
Later, when I heard that you were lost,

Your car found parked too near the bridge,
I wondered which of us had left it there.
By then I too was hanging from the edge.

OEUVRE

Will it ever be finished, this house
        Of paper
I began to raise when I was seventeen?

Others scramble from foundations far less firm.
        Seasons of
Pondering, name by name, the past's magnificent,

A squandering. Surely I might have lived.
        Spitefully
Watching as rivals stole the girls, got the jobs,

Won the laurels, the misery seeped in,
        Tinting the
Windows, darkening the fairest day.

But how should I have known, a house to please
        Need not be
Outlandish? And that searching everywhere

The fresh, the rare, prowling the gaudier
        Capitals,
Something of each would rub off, deface.

Well, we build where and as we can. There are
        Days when I
Am troubled by an image of the house,

Laden, rootless, like a tinseled tree,
        Suddenly
Torn to a thousand scribbled leaves and borne off

By the wind, then to be gathered and patched
        Whole again,
Or of the thing going up in smoke

And I, the paper dreamer, wide awake.

SNOW

Centuries
snow
has drifted
"feather like"
through poems,
so thick,
one on a ladder,
connoisseur
of snows,
archivist
of weathers,
gingerly raising
a ten-foot pen,
climbing
after it onto
that frozen waste,
would find
much snow,
little poetry.
Meanwhile
the writer,
after many weeks,
feels
his hand move —
now it stops,
a footprint artist
pausing
in the snow.

I.M. PABLO PICASSO
(for my father)

All is ordinary again —
in a thousand places,
convergences,

displaced parts flying
together: an ear,
a nose, a breast spinning

like a hand-grenade,
a third eye shot
with cloud, deep, staring,

and here, in Chicago
a great
flapping of wings.

PARIS

With fifty thousand daubers
To paint your face, you will never
Grow old, they say, with as many lovelies
Legging up your squares, you will
Always gratify, they say, O with your river
          And your bridges and your quays,
The mind need never wander to the north,
The east, the west, nor settle in the azured south,
          They say.

Yet ask any two Frenchmen
Spawned on the cobbles of whatever
Dreary *arrondissement*, ask them at the hour
The terraces are emptied of their tables,
The chairs piled high, the sidewalks scoured,
          And looking to the north, the east,
The west, finally to the brilliant
South, they'll say *Merde!* and *Merde!* again. That's what
          They say.

Ah, to one spawned on the asphalt
Of whatever American city, it is sweetest comfort
To know that, stripped of the décor, your gargoyles
          Pulled down (O hear the tourists sobbing in the choir!),
Bereft of the fifty thousand palettes and the
          Innumerable brushes that hide your face,
You are no more ugly than that garish
Daughter who, after plying fabulously the Champs Elysées,
          They say,

Ended up, five years later
Under a gaslight in Les Halles. *Zut alors!*
I'd rather be a banker in Duluth, with a Swede
          Wife and two cars in the garage, than a
Boulevardier with ten *sous* in the pocket, a head gone
          Soft with dreaming north, east, west, and south,
          And a kept bitch that cheers the porter in a
Greasy bed. *Mon Dieu! c'est triste la vie, n'est-ce pas?*
          They say.

MASK

Behind the tattered brow
    the skull looms sharp:
as branch survives its fruit
    and wind-picked bark,
so bone releases flesh
    to weather nakedly
and lone: on winter's frost
    burns summer's day.

LOVE POEM

Startle my wife again —
"Where will we lay our bones?"

Harmless, you'd think, yet
she's berserk. "Mere joshing,"

I protest. She will not
listen. I want an island

for us, apart, ringed with stones,
clusterings of flowers

merging us closer through
the all of time. She thinks

me mad with dreaming,
but it's love for her

which spurs me, this need
to know we'll never separate.

TWISTER

Waiting the twister which touched down
a county north, leveled a swath
of homes, taking twenty lives,

we sit in battered chairs, southwest
corner of the basement, listen
to the radio warnings through

linoleum and creaky floorboards
of the kitchen overhead. We are
like children in a spooky film,

ghosts about to enter at the door.
I try to comfort them, though
most afraid, *Survival Handbook*

open on my lap. Around our
piled up junk cobwebs sagged with flies,
though early spring. A trunk with French Line

stickers, paint flaked in our defective
furnace heat, a stack of dishes
judged too vulgar for our guests,

sled with rusted runners, cockeyed pram
and broken dolls, Christmas trinkets
we may use again, some boards kept

mainly for the nails. I watch my wife,
son, daughter, wondering what we're up to,
what's ahead. We listen, ever

silent, for the roar out of the west,
whatever's zeroing in with terror
in its wake. The all-clear sounds,

a pop song hits above. Made it
once again. We shove the chairs
against the wall, climb into the light.

THE CANNERY

In summer this town is full of rebels
Come up from Tennessee to shell the peas.

And wetbacks roam the supermarts, making
A Tijuana of the drab main street.

The Swedes and Poles who work at Wurlitzer,
And can't stand music, are all dug in:

Doors are bolted, their pretty children warned,
Where they wait for the autumnal peace.

At night the cannery's like a train,
A runaway, cans flung up like clinkers.

Sometimes on an evening hot as Southland
When even fear won't keep the windows down,

One hears the drawl of Tennessee, the quick
Laugh of Mexico in the empty streets.

WILLOWS
(for Taigan Takayama, Zen Master)

I was walking where the willows
ring the pond, meaning to reflect
on each, as never before, all
twenty-seven, examine twig by twig,
leaf by pointed leaf, those delicate
tents of greens and browns. I'd

tried before, but always wound up
at my leafless bole of spine, dead
ego stick, with its ambitions,
bothers, indignations. Times
I'd reach the fifth tree before
faltering, once the seventeenth.

Then, startled by grinding teeth,
sharp nails in the palm, turn back,
try again. Hoping this time to
focus on each bough, twig, leaf,
cast out all doubts that brought
me to the willows. This time

it would be different, could see
leaves shower from the farthest
tree, crown my head, bless my eyes,
when I awakened to the fact —
mind drifting to the trees ahead.
I was at fault again, stumbling to

the flap of duck, goose, a limping
footstep on the path behind,
sun-flash on the pond. Such excuse,
easy to find, whether by willows
or bristling stations of a life.
Once more, I'm off. This time

all's still. Alone, no one to blame
distractions on but self. Turn in
my tracks, back to the starting point.
Clench, unclench my hands, breathe in,
move off telling the leaves like
rosary-beads, willow to willow. Mind

clear, eye seeing all, and nothing.
By the fifth, leaves open to me,
touch my face. My gaze, in wonderment,
brushes the water. By the seventh,
know I've failed. Weeks now, I've been
practicing on my bushes, over, over again

PART THREE

Voyage: New Poems

WAR SONG

1

It was the moment summer
sounds breathless, drifts
into bittersweet autumn,

and the woody resonance
of poplars braced for winds
to come. And the tremor

of rushes sparked passion,
and mothers were laughing
and fathers aimed children

into the cloudless sky,
caught them giggling,
begging for more. Babies

blossomed, pulses of lovers
ticked over like restless
bees. Rumors came faster than

thoughts, and the news was war.

2

In the hush before
morning, amber of street
lamps, pinpricks of

stars, frantic dreams
slipped away, as light
swallowed darkness

through open windows
a desolate season of
chill air seeped in.

While fathers, sons,
lovers, spare kit in
duffles, marched down

the highroad, caught
in a maelstrom to
goodness knows where.

"Keep a stiff upper lip,"
they said, "back before
trees turn red." Lovers

were sighing, children were
whining, babies were fussing
because mothers were crying.

3

Leaves became draughts of
birds racing in bitter
wind, bare branches pointing

like fists clenched in grief.
But as the lull dawdled on,
weeks, months turned over,

and lovers wrote letters
till fingers were thumbs.
And mothers hummed once

again, kettles boiled shrilly,
babes suckled and burped
content as before. And

the children paraded, sticks
harnessed to shoulders.
They took sides and hated,

and took turns at killing,
then went home forgiven
because they were friends.

4

Columbines reared heads
in summer's kaleidoscope,
roses by hollyhocks scented

the day. The old with their
whispers of old wars
mulled over, while children

linked daisies and wore
them as crowns. Babes sleeping
in shade, smiled through cicada

chant. Mothers, lovers sought
news that would bring their
men home. It was then that

the warning came, rising
and falling, and bird song
was lost in the droning of

planes. Like comets of fire
and ice bombs were colliding.
Time splintered, walls

shattered, real war had come.
And as the smoke fizzled,
and fires were gutted, a hush

settled in. No mothers for
crying, no lovers for sighing,
no babies for fussing, no

children for whining.
                    And
soon through the rubble
wild flowers were blooming.

BLANK PAGE

What's to become
of it? Anything,
nothing? Could it

change the world?
Blot time from eyes,
ink through puddles

of pain, leaf by
the dead-letter office
of soul? Or race

over shadows of
Stinking Creek Road
by the Cumberland Gap

where fireflies lamp
a lone cat in a stand-
off with butterflies?

Could it change
with a comma, this
urge to fold over,

crease into a bird,
aim it soaring
through space forever?

WEB

Stumped for words
    I watch
the spider, nimble
    vagabond,

shuttle among twigs
    of the ever-
green. Its patience
    mesmerizes.

From my pen a thread
    crisscrosses
lines of silk into
    a geometric

sphere, a fragile cup,
    to filter
morning sun into
    my window,

frescoing the wall.

WOOLGATHERING

Caught in a web of
sweat and ginger, I
review day's efforts,

my butterfingered
phrases choking the
rubbish bin. Dream

I'm the Roman poet
Cinna, threatened by
the mob for my bad verse.

Want to escape this
twanging of the nerves,
find clear as silk

a brushstroke in the
sun. Rewind the music,
take a giant leap, backwards.

DOODLE

Ink flows beyond the first
range of hills, endlessly
follows a silent path. Slips

by the clutter of cities,
skirting pure landscape, down
to the ocean. Out of a blot,

tangled in wind, come a plaintive
gull song, an urgent whale call
rumbling throughout the deep.

The last cry of victims, lost
in the pull of a restless tide
that draws down images of planets,

like frail moths ringing the stars.

THE SEARCH

The stranger fast
approaching, as I
fill my eyes with

wild flowers, would
think me odd, weird,
daft, were I to offer

him my secret. Could
I trust him,
would he understand

this need to fashion
images of cocksfoot,
couplets from the

evening primrose, wring
music from a thistle?
As he passes, lifts

his hand in greeting,
I tell him nothing,
not a word.

SHRINE OF THE CRANE
(YAMAGUCHI, JAPAN)

Once, far back in time, moving
as slow shadows in a mime by
the stone lanterns, chipped,

discolored now, processions
of shrine maidens, vestal sprigs
crossed at their breasts, led

by stiff-robed priests, black
lacquered clogs tap-tapping on
the path, filed by worshippers

under red *toriis*, up stone steps,
passing three fox shrines aflush
with offerings, coins, rice cakes,

twigs embroidered with a paper-twist
of prayer. Today those hungry
ghosts with lofty dreams have fled

the hum of useless prayer on prayer,
to get ahead, outstrip, outdo,
all dreams lost somewhere in the fold

of time, deaf to the song of cranes.

VISITING MY FATHER

My father, who would take
his belt to me for telling
whoppers when I was a boy,
now whispers secrets on our

autumn walks. Daydreams
spill with leaves that
shimmy by us, freckling
the grass. Words leap from

the shadow of his 93-year
skirmish, become the bullet
searing through him on
the Western Front. Fame's

thrust upon him for his
sculpture of primeval man.
Cautiously I gesture where
geese fan over, ribboning

the sky. But lost in fancy
he unveils his monumental
visions in museums through
the world. Turning by remnants

of blue asters, chicory and
Queen Anne's lace, we hug
farewell. He stares into my
eyes, assuring me that dons

of Oxford, Moscow, the Sorbonne
call daily for his expertise.
Driving home, I pull up for
a field mouse, watch him dart

back into ripened corn. Passing
a stand of maple canopies,
I need to touch, hold onto,
run my fingers through their gold.

BLACK BEAN SOUP

I shadow the pond
patient as stone, catch
the sadness of wind
carving seashells

in traces of snow
in the park. Last
night, found my wife
sobbing at words in

her crossword puzzle.
There it was —
Black Bean Soup. And
there was my father,

months before dying,
asking in, out of
shadows for black
bean soup. My sister

and I watched him
leaving us slowly. My
thoughts back in time,
nearly seventy years,

tramping through snow,
hands clasped, off
to the park. "Snow,"
he said. "Snow," I said.

Laughing together, sliding
back home. Stamping
feet on the doormat,
eager for mother's good

soup, rich and thick.
Light and dark are memories,
like mountain junipers
snared by the kudzu,

ghosts for all time.
A tabby, half cocked
on a garden wall, shakes
off snowflakes, springs

down, rubs against me
like an old friend
as I pass. In spite of
death the winter cherry

blooms. A bird flies sharp
against the chill gray sky.

WAITING FOR THE LIGHT

They have laid down their
plowshares: mile upon mile
along Quentin Road villas

blossom on richest soil in
the U.S.A. New developments —
Goose Cove, *Hunter's Creek*,

Willow Bend — sprout where
the corn grew so high. Pulling
up as the light turns red

on the corner of Route 22,
by a woodframe house, man, woman
and boy are having it out on

the lawn. The man shakes his
fist, the woman reacts in kind,
the boy, hoarse with outrage,

runs inside, slamming the door.
As the light changes, I rev off
into what's left of the day.

ON THE WAY TO ROCKFORD

On the scenic route down
Cherry Valley Road in a freak
blizzard, windshield wipers

stropping at the ice — squinting
at glazed branches doodling
the backdrop of the sky, I slow

down as I come upon the tipsied
farmhouse, county eyesore,
rubbish heap of skeletal barn,

sheds, car parts, rusted tractor,
pickup, now phantom sculptures
under snow. No sign of the old

man, who in summer basks with
dog, cat, chickens on his sinking
stoop, a lone philosopher. As

I pass by a cow stares upward
from the frozen patch, a curtain
in an upstairs window moves.

REVERIE

Caught in the song
of playgrounds,
drifts of children's
voices coil like smoke.

I pass, yet cannot
leave these joyous
rousers. Glance back
over my shoulder,

remembering the hit
and run of time.
Spinning my son, my
daughter, then my

grandson, faster,
faster on the roundabout
near primrose banks
and bluebell woods,

where I, a child
among them, orbit
through trees chained
together by the sun.

APRIL SHOWERS

Sheer gray beauty, clouds
move in and out the day,
drive brushstrokes of rain
along the gutters, drenching

me, and the old wino guzzling
daily by the corner church,
chuckling to himself, foul-
mouthing passers by. Today

he starts out hunched over
a puddle, stirring rainbows
with his walking stick.
Uninvited witness, I clear

off before he ferrets out
my need to stir up colors of
the street — his boozy flush,
prisms of laburnum, almond,

cherry blossoms, misted bluebells,
iridescent songbirds. Rustling
the bold wash of spring
into a rainbow of my very own.

STUDENT

Oddly, the lone sound
of the white stick
steers the blind girl
through the classroom

door. The look behind
her eyes, a poem-in-waiting.
Running her fingers over,
fine-tuning lines of

Yeats's "Second Coming,"
she stares into a void
strung out with stars.
And the miracle comes

as she reads out slowly,
softly, voice rising with
passion, music caught up
in the wind, leaving the room

in a silence richly dark.

AND STILL BIRDS SING

1. Snapshots

Here we are together, clearing
out the past: old letters,
cuttings, photographs, crossing
our palm with memories, rich

as wildflowers, making room for
what will be, sum of our ups
and downs. Naked as shadows under
a waterfall of rose and silver

flashing between clouds, we stumble
in and out forgotten streets. Wonder:
Where's this? What's that? Fingering
images of loved ones, slipped by

sudden as a downburst, fleeter than
dancers waiting the last flute call.
Stare back over shoulders, as time
unraveling like silk leads us through

a path of broom, thrift and forget-
me-nots, where goodbys are forever.
Hold onto those we thought would
never leave, our children grown and gone.

Recall with belly-laughs the antics of
our son, our daughter and our grandson.
Within the filigree of borders follow
them to where their dreams have led.

Among the orange grass, cornflowers,
harebells, cowslips, ochre mountains
of our treks we stare in silence
at an irreplaceable light.

2. Newspaper Cuttings

Why did we keep these items, these
reports of World War II, these horror
stories of the living dead, eyes burning
through barbed wire? Still, those

tortured ones, men, women, children
moved from nightmare, kissed the hands
of liberators. Why did we save this
grim account of bodies of young soldiers

in Vietnam, piled high in an oxcart,
waiting the last lap of their journey
home? And still sun shone. We smooth
out headlines of a twister that wiped out

a town, rode trees and homes like thistledown
across the highway, left survivors
wandering in an alien place. Still, they
sifted rubble for the pieces that made up

their lives. We open up a page, stare
at the orphans in the ruins of Chechnya
huddled together, and the copy reads,
"They sing to calm the night." Nearby

a little girl points to a woman, face down
in the mud, says, "That's my mother.
Can you bury her?" Death offered up no
sound. And still birds sang. We feel

the need to leave this trail of pain, this
ravaging history. Take a rest from wounds
of deep reopened scars. Let poems tumbleweed
by cornfields turned to lakes in a new flood,

trees richened by rains, wildflowers run
a-riot from these flashfloods out of season.
Together, we ride by the periwinkle blue
of chicory, Queen Anne's lace, and yellow

asters in soft grasses, tiger lilies, goldenrod
and trumpet vines, clusters of sunflowers,
vetch and mustard, and we wonder at
the cruelty in such a lovely world.

3. Letters

Reading them, remembrance takes off
like clear paw prints in the snow.
Voices overwhelm us — a litany of
family and friends drawn as a thrum

of bees, nudging our hearts, muddling
with us through the ebb and flow of years,
searching the letter-box for fragments
we clung onto, like cockleburs, which

stirred up cravings for more news on
fragile paper, proof of our yesterdays.
We look into each other's eyes. We
cannot clear them out, will have to find

another corner for what's yet to come.
Replace them where we found them,
snapshots, cuttings, letters. Through the
open windows feel the season changing, once

again leaves turning in autumn, squirrels
gallivanting in the branches, and
the cat across the way crouched in the
bushes, set to pounce. And still birds sing.

SHOPPING

On our weekly jaunt into
the supermart my wife and I
part company among the green-
groceries — the martyr in me
takes his punishment without
a gripe. While she pokes
at bananas, veg, finecombs
a lettuce, chooses her iris,
daffodils, a bit of green,
I traipse along the aisles,
outflanking pushcarts, dodging
elbows, baskets. Steer by
baked beans, brooms, sultanas,
marmalade and nuts, All Bran,
pickled cabbage. Passing the
cat and dog food I'm confronted
by a man who seems to know me,
plasters me against the toilet
paper and begins the complex
story of his life. By now my
wife is going through the check-
out. I try to get a word in
while he's through with affair
number three and coming up to
four. I take my courage in my
hands, tell him I've got to go.
Take off, heave bags into our
old car's trunk as he comes up
behind me to conclude his tale.
Says, "What's your name again?"
Then, with a puzzled frown —
"Hey, do I know you?"

MEDITATION

Morning at my desk as the first
whirligig of light springs me
from my reverie — the canvas
of my mind fills with the brick

wall of the offices across
the way, windows phosphorescing,
and the face. Curtains parted,
eyes monitor my every smudge

that taps into those earphones,
scrambles the computer. I sit
here with my pen, aware we are
communicators in a fragile world

where ravaged towns and villages
glow red as berries on
the mountain ash, before the
daylight, swallowed, draws us close.

PIGEON IN THE RAIN

On my morning jaunt
across Queen Mary's Garden
I wait in pelting rain
before a flash of pigeons

settles in my path.
Preening feathers, sorting
through the bushes,
unruffled by the absent

feeders bearing crumbs
in plastic bags. A
gallivanter puffs his
breast, vibrates in

courtship, scorned by
one, another. He's
content to turn tail
on the roses, flit

from branch to trellis,
drift through the
downpour toward clouds,
fly into my poem.

COLONEL MUSTARD

I pass the old man cranking
up his record player on
the pavement, in all weathers,
tap-dancing on the spot,

faster in winter, slow in
this sultry heat. Head bent
under a frayed bowler, eyes
shifting, following the feet

skedaddling by —
"Any small change, please?"
Emptiness flows through the ink-
brush of ideas, fills spaces

in between clouds, and shoes
beating to a cranked-out tune.
And eyes insisting life's
a cock-up in a bleak and lonely

corner, where people do not
stop to mingle with the living
dead, but turn their faces
sharply from his stage. Since

pity's not enough, his taps
hurl spears into the crowds.
His drama fills their day —
"Any small change, please?"

LONDON MATINÉE

Three strangers at the bus stop,
walk-ons in a farce, squint
into distance, lines best forgotten.

Road a blank script, no cue forthcoming:
posters, like backdrops, staging
an image. Framed in the shadows,

leading to nowhere, three strangers
at the bus stop, newspapers underarm —
promise of scenes to come: violence,

dreams gone sour, love-twists, freak
blizzards, wars in the distance. They
eye one another, marooned in a silence.

DELIVERY

Here he comes, the postman,
destiny in his sack: bill, ad,
bungled address, ritual of

acceptance or denial. The
tearing open on relief, on pain,
the send up of frustration

pencilled in the dark museum
of the brain. Sit back on
my heels, watch his shadow

close in on the door. No wish
to confront him — blame
the messenger for all he drops

into my letter box, all he does not.

AIRING NEW SHOES

My Sears 440
joggers on
the flagstones

by the hedge
reek of
formaldehyde,

send ant tribes
into exile
under violets

in the grass.
Birds hover,
will not light

near the offending
twosome that
will take me

rigged and sweaty
on my lick-split
round the park.

BOSNIA

Trees still bend in the winds
of Bosnia, while the fool's-harvest
of death is tallied each day.

As the candle burns down, and the
ritual of living goes on, shops
open and close, mosques, churches

are filled. The pot simmers,
as if awaiting the footsteps of
children out playing in snow —

soon to become silent snow angels
caught in bitter games of their
fathers, where in a pitiless landscape

nobody wins and the rules are not fair.
And we watch as the generals carp and
the victims bleed on the ten o'clock news.

DOCUDRAMA

So many ways to suffer:
cast-offs, no-names, orphans
of Bogota run with rats,

lice-ridden dogs, scabied cats,
leery of the TV special
panning the great Cathedral,

trendy streets. They swarm from
hiding places, collar purses,
rip through cars, swiping their

daily bread from well-stocked
shelves. Merchants, swanky
shoppers, transfixed as a mural

drying on the wall, wait on the
death squad bullets to pick them
off like flies, bursting the bubble

of their bitter world. Blood,
a tear or so, shine on the stones,
frozen forever in a camera's eye.

THE ROUND

Slowly, dark through
the sycamore shadows

the window, fuzzes wind-
dodging birds set down

in its branches. I listen
in wonder to icicles

chiming night rituals of
winter. Wait for dawn's

whirl-spin of light
and the shiver of wings.

FOR HELEN, ON HER BIRTHDAY

Somewhere, among wildflowers
        in a quiet place,
as yet undredged, untrampled,
        dearest,

is the small mound that one
        day will hold
a scrap of granite bearing
        our poor name.

When footsteps of our children,
        and their children
fade, do not despair. We will
        have begun

another journey into the unknown,
        content
as always, holding tightly
        to each other.

VOYAGE

1

That was the year midsummer's
heatwave knocked us all
for loops: cats, squirrels

up, down, round the oak and
sycamore, mobbed the birdbath,
scratched in frenzy at the camel-

back packed earth. Birds veered
cockeyed, whomped the kitchen
window. Grass snakes frizzled

on the concrete path. That
was the year mosquitoes
failed to guzzle, as I drifted

by the parched Kishwaukee river,
caught up with my wife
and daughter for a turn around

the park.
                   Faltered as I
stepped down from the bridge.

2

That was the year the paramedics
strapped me in the helicopter,
pointed me to stars, in fits

and starts between the cockleburs
of galaxies, my eyes blurred up
with ghosts of mayhem, fireflies,

outcasts sifting garbage on hot
city streets. That was the year
on hold. Riddled with lifelines

in an alien bed, I thumbed the Sunday
bookpage, stared at faces of those
Auschwitz children waiting a turn

upon the Zyklon carrousel — near
the last photograph of Primo Levi,
their fire-eyed witness, before

he took his life,
                   slamming
the door on half a century's pain.

3

And this year, botched up
once again, oxygen mask in
place, heart monitor intact,

cut off from warzone static,
buzz and scuttle of the
misery out there. My wife,

my dearest friend, stroked
the blue flower round
the IV in my arm, coaxed

darkness from my eyes.
With tapestries of words
sent acrobatic sparrows

rising like last autumn's
leaves from fresh-turned soil,
wove flocks of scarlet tanagers

above gold-sovereign dandelions,
unthreaded winter hair of
willows greening into spring.

And this year, back full
circle in the summer heat,
I know for all it lacks

this world is still the only
place, and walking in a flame
of sunset I have things to do.

PART FOUR

Zen Translations: Introduction
Chinese Poems of Enlightenment and Death

ZEN TRANSLATIONS
Introduction

Apart from the haiku, long associated with Zen, the poems that follow
were written by Chinese and Japanese Zen masters and laymen from
the eighth century to the present. The poems are so suggestive in
themselves that explication is rarely necessary; furthermore, the poets
rarely theorized about the poems they would write from time to time,
and for good reason: to them poetry was not, as so often in the West,
an art to be cultivated but a means by which an attempt at the nearly
inexpressible could be made. Though certain of the poems are called
satori (enlightenment) and others death poems, in a sense all Zen poetry
deals with momentous experience. There are, in other words, no finger
exercises, and though some of the poems may seem comparatively
light, there is not one that is not totally in earnest, fully inspired.
Indeed when you consider the Zenist's traditional goal, the all-or-nothing
quality of his striving after illumination, this is scarcely to be wondered
at. The Zen state of mind has been described as "one in which the
individual identifies with an object without any sense of restraint," as
in this poem by Bunan:

> The moon's the same old moon,
> The flowers exactly as they were,
> Yet I've become the thingness
> Of all the things I see!

Zen poetry is highly symbolic, and the moon here is a common symbol.
It should be remembered, in relation to the use of such symbols, that
Zen is a Mahayana school, and that the Zenist searches, always within
himself, for the indivisible moon reflected not only on the sea but on
each dew drop. To discover this, the Dharmakaya, in all things is for
the Zenist to discover his own Buddha-nature. Perhaps most Zen poems,
whether designated as such or not, are satori poems, which are
composed immediately after an awakening and are presented to a
master for approval. Daito's poem is typical:

At last I've broken Unmon's barrier!
There's exit everywhere — east, west; north, south.
In at morning, out at evening; neither host nor guest.
My every step stirs up a little breeze.

And here is a satori poem by Eichu:

> My eyes eavesdrop on their lashes!
> I'm finished with the ordinary!
> What use has halter, bridle
> To one who's shaken off contrivance?

Traditionally death poems are written or dictated by Zenists right before death. The author looks back on his life and, in a few highly compressed lines, expresses his state of mind at the inevitable hour. The following are among the best known:

FUMON

> Magnificent! Magnificent!
> No-one knows the final word.
> The ocean bed's aflame,
> Out of the void leap wooden lambs.

KUKOKU

> Riding this wooden upside-down horse,
> I'm about to gallop through the void.
> Would you seek to trace me?
> Ha! Try catching the tempest in a net.

ZEKKAI

> The void has collapsed upon the earth,
> Stars, burning, shoot across Iron Mountain.
> Turning a somersault, I brush past.

The void, mentioned in all three of these death poems, is the great Penetralium of Zen. The mind, it is thought, is a void in which objects are stripped of their objectivity and reduced to their essence. In the death poem which follows, by Bokuo, there is an important Zen symbol, the ox, which here serves as an object of discipline:

> For seventy-two years
> I've kept the ox well under.
> Today, the plum in bloom again,
> I let him wander in the snow.

Bokuo, in his calm acceptance of death, proves himself a true Zen-man. Though satori and death figure heavily in Zen poetry, most of the poems deal with nature and man's place in it. Simply put, the Buddha-nature is by no means peculiar to man. It is discoverable in all that exists, animate or inanimate. Perhaps in this poem by Ryokan the Zen spirit is perfectly caught:

> Without a jot of ambition left
> I let my nature flow where it will.
> There are ten days of rice in my bag
> And, by the hearth, a bundle of firewood.
> Who prattles of illusion or nirvana?
> Forgetting the equal dusts of name and fortune,
> Listening to the night rain on the roof of my hut,
> I sit at ease, both legs stretched out.

The mountain — Buddha's body.
The torrent — his preaching.
Last night, eighty-four thousand poems.
How, how make them understand?
                    LAYMAN SOTOBA (1036-1101)

How long the tree's been barren.
At its tip long ropes of cloud.
Since I smashed the mud-bull's horns,
The stream's flowed backwards.
                                        HOGE

On the rocky slope, blossoming
Plums — from where?
Once he saw them, Reiun
Danced all the way to Sandai.
                                    HOIN

No dust speck anywhere.
What's old? new?
At home on my blue mountain,
I want for nothing.
                              SHOFU

Loving old priceless things,
I've scorned those seeking
Truth outside themselves:
Here, on the tip of the nose.
                    LAYMAN MAKUSHO

A deafening peal,
A thief escaped
My body. What
Have I learnt?
The Lord of Nothingness
Has a dark face.
                    LAYMAN YAKUSAI

The mountain slopes crawl with lumberjacks,
Axing everything in sight —
Yet crimson flowers
Burn along the stream.
                         CHIN-DOBA

All's harmony, yet everything is separate.
Once confirmed, mastery is yours.
Long I hovered on the Middle Way,
Today the very ice shoots flame.
                         CHOKEI (d. 932)

I was born with a divine jewel,
Long since filmed with dust.
This morning, wiped clean, it mirrors
Streams and mountains, without end.
                         IKUZANCHU

Does one really have to fret
About enlightenment?
No matter what road I travel,
I'm going home.

SHINSHO

When Master Ungo asked,
"What is it comes?" I danced for joy.
Though one grasps it on the spot,
One's still buried alive.

ZUIGAN, 10C.

I'm twenty-seven years
And always sought the Way.
Well, this morning we passed
Like strangers on the road.

KOKUIN, 10C.

Iron will's demanded of
The student of the Way —
It's always on the mind.
Forget all — good, bad.
Suddenly it's yours.

RIJUNKYOKU, 11C.

The stone mortar rushes through the air,
The golden lion turns into a dog.
Is it the North Star you reach for?
Fold hands behind the South.

YOOKU

Until today the precious gem's been buried,
Now it flashes from the earth. Mind's clear
At last. Zen-sitting, a stick of incense
Lights the universe. I bow to Bodhidharma.

RYOZAN, 10C.

This grasped, all's dust —
The sermon for today.
Lands, seas. Awakened,
You walk the earth alone.

SEIGENSAI, 12C.

Forget everything — everything!
Now from the path the night bell
Tinkling. Is that the moon
At the bottom of the pool?
The mud bull shatters against the coral.

TOSU, 12C.

There I was, hunched over office desk,
Mind an unruffled pool.
A thunderbolt! My middle eye
Shot wide, revealing — my ordinary self.

LAYMAN SEIKEN, 11C.

One question, and master thunders.
Mount Sumeru hides in the Big Dipper,
Billows cover the very sky.
Here's a nose. A mouth.

KYOCHU, 12C.

Seventy-six: done
With this life —
I've not sought heaven,
Don't fear hell.
I'll lay these bones
Beyond the Triple World,
Unenthralled, unperturbed.
           FUYO-DOKAI (1042-1117)

Sixty-five years,
Fifty-seven a monk.
Disciples, why ask
Where I'm going,
Nostrils to earth?
           UNPO BUN-ETSU

Don't tell me how difficult the Way.
The bird's path, winding far, is right
Before you. Water of the Dokei Gorge,
You return to the ocean, I to the mountain.
                    HOFUKU SEIKATSU, 10C.

For eighty years I've talked of east and west:
What nonsense. What's long/short? big/small?
There's no need of the gray old man, I'm one
With all of you, in everything. Once through
The emptiness of all, who's coming? Who going?
                         KIYO, 8C.

All Patriarchs are above our understanding,
And they don't last forever.
O my disciples, examine, examine.
What? Why this. This only.

BEIREI, 8C.

I've remained in Mokuchin thirty years.
In all that time not one disciplinary merit.
If asked why Bodhidharma came from the West
I'll say, unknitting my brow — "What's that?"

MOKUCHIN JURO, 9C.

This year turning sixty-four, elements
About to dissolve within me — the Path!
A miracle of miracles, yet where
The Buddhas and Patriarchs? No need
To shave my head again, or wash.
Just set the firewood flaming — that's enough.

NANGAKU GENTAI, 9C.

Light dies in the eyes, hearing
Fades. Once back to the Source,
There's no special meaning —
Today, tomorrow.

ETSUZAN, 10C.

The Mount Sumeru mallet firmly gripped,
I pound through the drum of space.
Hiding, I leave not a trace —
Behold the snared sun!

SHONEN (1215-1289)

PART FIVE

Poems of Japanese Masters

Firm on the seven Buddhas' cushion,
Center, center. Here's the armrest
My master handed down. Now, to it!
Head up, eyes straight, ears in line with shoulders.

DOGEN (1200-1253)

WAKA ON THE CORRECT-LAW EYE TREASURY

There in midnight water,
Waveless, windless,
The old boat's swamped
With moonlight.

DOGEN

WAKA

Mind's no solid
One can touch or see —
Dew, frost.

DOGEN

WAKA ON ZEN SITTING

Scarecrow in the hillock
Paddy field —
How unaware! How useful!

DOGEN

WAKA ON IMPERMANENCE

The world? Moonlit
Drops shaken
From the crane's bill.

DOGEN

WAKA ON KYOSEI'S RAINDROP SOUND

As he listened,
Mindlessly,
The eavesdrops entered him.

DOGEN

I'm but a festering lump,
Most bestial of humans.
Years I've walked Chinese fashion,
Barefoot. Straw sandals
Brand-new, I touch my nose.

EJO (1198-1280)

Saddled as everyone with karma,
Who can deny the Buddha-mind within?
Ever yoked, yet not a glimpse of him.
At last I've tracked him down: myself.

TETTSU (1219-1309)

140

Eyes blinded by three poisons,
Yet once all ties are cut,
How restful. Wicker hat donned,
Cane held firm, how vast the sky!

UNGO (1583-1659)

WAKA

Careful! Even moonlit dewdrops,
If you're lured to watch,
Are a wall before the Truth.

SOGYO (1667-1731)

Eighty years, a day's journey.
I've lived everywhere, and now
The spring breeze doesn't try my door.
Snow lies heavy on my head.

GUAN, 18C.

CROSSING LAKE BIWA

Riding rain, astride wind, my plain robe light,
For ten *ri* the boat carries me across.
Hoisting sail, one knows how strong the wind.
The current tries both stem and stern.
Above the lake, mountains everywhere, among
The waves, in all directions, phantom paths.
A monk on a reed boat? And this not Futsu?
Ridiculous! Where is my Buddha-mind?

GEPPA, (b. 1664.)

Disciplined by wind and snow,
The Way of Reinan opens.
Look where — moon high, plums a-bloom —
The temple's fixed in stillness.

EUN (1232-1301)

Right's fine, wrong's fine —
There's nothing to nirvana,
And what's "defilement"?
Snowflake in the flame.

GUDO (1579-1661)

Spring come again, after moody
Wintering indoors, I left the hermitage
With begging bowl. The village children
Played in long-awaited sun. I bounced
Ball with them, chanting —
One-two-three-four-five-six-seven.
They bounced while I sang, they sang
While I bounced. So I've wasted,
Joyfully, a whole spring day.

RYOKAN (1757-1831)

JAPANESE HAIKU

To the willow —
all hatred, and desire
of your heart.
        BASHO (1644-1694)

Come, see
real flowers
of this painful world.
                BASHO

Wintry day,
on my horse
a frozen shadow.
        BASHO

Autumn moon,
tide foams
to the very gate.
                BASHO

Cedar umbrella,
off to Mount Yoshino
for the cherry blossoms.
            BASHO

Autumn —
even the birds
and clouds look old.
                BASHO

Year's end,
all corners
of this floating world, swept.
                    BASHO

Sick on a journey —
over parched fields
dreams wander on.
                    BASHO

Summer grasses,
all that remains
of soldiers' dreams.
                    BASHO

A sudden chill —
in our room my dead wife's
comb, underfoot.
                    BUSON (1715-1783)

My village —
dragonflies,
worn white walls.
                    BUSON

In sudden flare
of the mosquito wick,
her flushed face.
                    BUSON

Mountains of Yoshino —
shedding petals,
swallowing clouds.

BUSON

Cherry blossoms?
In these parts
grass also blooms.

ISSA (1763-1827)

Listen,
all creeping things —
the bell of transience.

ISSA

Don't weep, insects —
lovers, stars themselves,
must part.

ISSA

Where there are humans
you'll find flies,
and Buddhas.

ISSA

Let's take
the duckweed way
to clouds.

ISSA

First cicada:
life is
cruel, cruel, cruel.
                    ISSA

When plum
blooms —
a freeze in hell.
                    ISSA

I'm leaving —
now you can make love,
my flies.
                    ISSA

Nightingale's song
this morning,
soaked with rain.
                    ISSA

Children,
don't harm the flea,
with children.
                    ISSA

Autumn wind —
mountain's shadow
wavers.
                    ISSA

Watch it — you'll bump
your heads
on that stone, fireflies.

ISSA

Never forget:
we walk on hell,
gazing at flowers.

ISSA

In this world
even butterflies
must earn their keep.

ISSA

First firefly,
why turn away —
it's Issa.

ISSA

Under cherry trees
there are
no strangers.

ISSA

Imagine —
the monk took off
before the moon shone.

SHIKI (1867-1902)

Thing long forgotten —
pot where a flower blooms,
this spring day.

SHIKI

Autumn wind:
gods, Buddha —
lies, lies, lies.

SHIKI

Among Saga's
tall weeds,
tombs of fair women.

SHIKI

Such silence:
snow tracing wings
of mandarin ducks.

SHIKI

A WOOD IN SOUND

The pinetree sways in the smoke,
Which streams up and up.
There's a wood in sound.

My legs lose themselves
Where the river mirrors daffodils
Like faces in a dream.

A cold wind and the white memory
Of a sasanqua.
Warm rain comes and goes.

I'll wait calmly on the bank
Till the water clears
And willows start to bud.

Time is singed on the debris
Of air raids.
Somehow, here and now, I am another.

BACKYARD

The sky clears after rain,
Yellow roses glistening in the light.
Crossing two thresholds, the cat moves off.

Your back is overgrown with nandin leaves.
How awkward your gait!
Like a chicken on damp leaves.
Your necktie, made from skin
Of a tropical fighting fish,
Is hardly subdued. Your yolk-colored
Coat will soon be dyed
With blood again, like a cock's crest.

Let your glances pierce
Like a hedgehog's spines,
I reject them. I can't imagine
What would happen if our glances met.

One day I'll pulverize you.
Now you're scratching
In the bamboo roots, famished.
Watch it — I'll toss you down a hole.

With your cockspurs you kick off
Mars, earth, mankind,
All manner of things, then
Pick over them with your teeth.

Atomic horses bulge through
The pores of a peach-like girl.
The persimmon's leaves are gone again.

RED WAVES

A cat, a black-white tabby out of nowhere,
Licks its back at the water's edge:
Perhaps — with that bit of metal dangling
From her middle — a space cat,
Readying to fly off again.

But how to ask her? I opened my hand, wide,
Just in front of her face, at which
She flipped over, legs up and pointing
Toward the sea in the pose of a 'beckoning cat'.

The sea obliged: she was carried off
Bobbing on the waves. Was she drowned?
I asked myself over and over,
Alone for hours on the moonlit beach.

Suddenly a red parasol came rolling
Toward me — the cat's? It danced along
The windless shore, with me chasing full tilt.
I didn't have a chance. Come daybreak
I spotted the parasol rising above a rock:
The sun, blinding! Red waves reached my ankles.

THISTLES

Thistles bloomed in the vast moonlit
Cup of the Mexican sands.

Thistles bloomed on the round hillock
Of a woman's heart.

The stained sea was choked with thistles,
Sky stowed away in thistle stalks.

Thistles, resembling a male corpse, bloomed
Like murex from a woman's side.

At the thorny root of a yellow cactus plant
A plucked pigeon crouched,

And off in the distance a dog whimpered,
As if swallowing hot air.

BURNING ONESELF TO DEATH

That was the best moment of the monk's life.
Firm on a pile of firewood
With nothing more to say, hear, see,
Smoke wrapped him, his folded hands blazed.

There was nothing more to do, the end
Of everything. He remembered, as a cool breeze
Streamed through him, that one is always
In the same place, and that there is no time.

Suddenly a whirling mushroom cloud rose
Before his singed eyes, and he was a mass
Of flame. Globes, one after another, rolled out,
The delighted sparrows flew round like fire balls.

THE PIPE

While I slept it was all over,
Everything. My eyes, squashed white,
Flowed off toward dawn.

There was a noise,
Which, like all else, spread and disappeared:
There's nothing worth seeing, listening for.

When I woke, everything seemed cut off.
I was a pipe, still smoking,
Which daylight would knock empty once again.

WHAT IS MOVING

When I turned to look back
Over the waters
The sky was birdless.

Men *were, are* born.
Do I still live? I ask myself,
Munching a sweet potato.

Don't smell of death,
Don't cast its shadow.
Any woman when I glance her way,
Looks down,
Unable to stand it.
Men, as if dead,
Turn up the whites of their eyes.

Get rid of those trashy ideas —
The same thing
Runs through both of us.
My thought moves the world:
I move, it moves.
I crook my arm, the world's crooked.

153

WIND AMONG THE PINES

The wind blows hard among the pines
Toward the beginning
Of an endless past.
Listen: you've heard everything.

AFTERIMAGES

The volcanic smoke of Mount Aso
Drifted across the sea, white ash
Clinging to mulberry leaves
And crowning the heads of sparrows.

An open-mouthed lava crocodile;
A sparrow like a fossil sprig,
The moon filling its eyes;
A colossal water lizard stuck to a dead tree,
Its headland tail quaking.

A cloud floats in my head — beautiful!
When the sparrow opens its eyes,
Nothing but rosy space. All else gone.

Don't tell me that tree was red —
The only thing that moved, ever closer,
Was a girl's nose. All mere afterimages.

Water, coldness itself, flows underfoot.

The sparrow, eyes half closed, lay in an urn
In the pit. Now it fans up. The earth's
Fiery column is nearly extinguished.

QUAILS

It is the grass that moves, not the quails.
Weary of embraces, she thought of
Committing her body to the flame.

When I shut my eyes, I hear far and wide
The air of the Ice Age stirring.
When I open them, a rocket passes over a meteor.

A quail's egg is complete in itself,
Leaving not room enough for a dagger's point.
All the phenomena in the universe: myself.

Quails are supported by the universe
(I wonder if that means subsisting by God.)
A quail has seized God by the neck

With its black bill, because there is no
God greater than a quail.
(Peter, Christ, Judas: a quail.)

A quail's egg: idle philosophy in solution.
(There is no wife better than a quail.)
I dropped a quail's egg into a cup for buckwheat noodles,

And made havoc of the Democratic Constitution.
Split chopsticks stuck in the back, a quail husband
Will deliver dishes on a bicycle, anywhere.

The light yellow legs go up the hill of Golgotha.
Those quails who stood on the rock, became the rock!
The nightfall is quiet, but inside the congealed exuviae

Numberless insects zigzag, on parade.

THE POSITION OF THE SPARROW

The sparrow has cut the day in half:
Afternoons — yesterday's, the day after tomorrow's —
Layer the white wall.
Those of last year, and next year's too,
Are dyed into the wall — see them? —
And should the wall come down,
Why, those afternoons will remain,
Glimmering, just as they are, through time.
(That was a colorless realm where,
Nevertheless, most any color could well up.)

Just as the swan becomes a crow,
So everything improves — everything:
No evil *can* persist, and as to things,
Why, nothing is unchangeable.
The squirrel, for instance, is on the tray,
Buffalos lumber through African brush,
The snail wends along the wall,
Leaving a silver trail.
The sparrow's bill grips a pomegranate seed:
Just anything can resemble a lens, or a squirrel.

Because the whole is part, there's not a whole,
Anywhere, that is not part.
And all those happenings a billion years ago,
Are happening now, all around us: time.
Indeed this morning the sparrow hopped about
In that nebulous whirlpool
A million light years hence.

And since the morning is void,
Anything can be. Since mornings
A billion years from now are nothingness,
We can behold them.
The sparrow stirs,
The universe moves slightly.

CANNA

A red canna blooms,
While between us flickers
A death's head, dancing there
Like a pigmy or tiny ball.

We try to catch it —
Now it brushes my hands,
Now dallies with her feet.

She often talks of suicide.
Scared, I avoid her cold face.

Again today she spoke
Of certain premonitions.
How can I possibly
Save this woman's life?

Living as if dead, I shall
Give up my own. She must live.

DESTRUCTION

The universe is forever falling apart —
No need to push the button,
It collapses at a finger's touch:
Why, it barely hangs on the tail of a sparrow's eye.

The universe is so much eye secretion,
Hordes leap from the tips
Of your nostril hairs. Lift your right hand:
It's in your palm. There's room enough
On the sparrow's eyelash for the whole.

A paltry thing, the universe:
Here is all strength, here the greatest strength.
You and the sparrow are one
And, should he wish, he can crush you.
The universe trembles before him.

THE PEACH

A little girl under a peach tree,
Whose blossoms fall into the entrails
Of the earth.

There you stand, but a mountain may be there
Instead; it is not unlikely that the earth
May be yourself.

You step against a plate of iron and half
Your face is turned to iron. I will smash
Flesh and bone

And suck the cracked peach. She went up the mountain
To hide her breasts in the snowy ravine.
Women's legs

Are more or less alike. The leaves of the peach tree
Stretch across the sea to the end of
The continent.

The sea was at the little girl's beck and call.
I will cross the sea like a hairy
Caterpillar

And catch the odor of your body.

RAIN

The rain keeps falling,
Even in dreams.
The skull leaks badly.

There's a constant dripping
Down the back.
The rain, which no one

Remembers starting,
Keeps falling,
Even on the finest days.

STITCHES

My wife is always knitting, knitting:
Not that I watch her,
Not that I know what she thinks.

(Awake till dawn
I drowned in your eyes —
I must be dead:
Perhaps it's the mind that stirs.)

With that bamboo needle
She knits all space, piece by piece,
Hastily hauling time in.

Brass-cold, exhausted,
She drops into bed and,
Breathing calmly, falls asleep.

Her dream must be deepening,
Her knitting comes loose.

FISH

I hold a newspaper, reading.
Suddenly my hands become cow ears,
Then turn into Pusan, the South Korean port.

Lying on a mat
Spread on the bankside stones,
I fell asleep.
But a willow leaf, breeze-stirred,
Brushed my ear.
I remained just as I was,
Near the murmurous water.

When young there was a girl
Who became a fish for me.
Whenever I wanted fish
Broiled in salt, I'd summon her.
She'd get down on her stomach
To be sun-cooked on the stones.
And she was always ready!

Alas, she no longer comes to me.
An old benighted drake,
I hobble homeward.
But look, my drake feet become horse hoofs!
Now they drop off
And, stretching marvelously,
Become the tracks of the Tokaido Railway Line.

PIGEON

The pigeon sleeps with half-closed eyes.
Opened, they fill with azaleas
And space expands before them.
There are white plum blossoms like little faces,
A milky fog about the sun.
The pigeon's no solid, not one or two.

Curiously the red camellia has both stamen, pistil,
And in the mother's dim shrunken bosom a million
        babies,
Hair tips glistening, green necks glittering,
Are like pigeons taking wing.

Yet those eyes are sightless, turned in,
And the bed sheets are like ink stains
Blurred with babies,
To be wiped clean by the mother's numberless wings.

Now is the time of hydrangeas,
And yellow butterflies flit into the mother's mind,
While the gray pigeons, flying helter skelter,
Cannot escape, drop onto the shoulder of the atomic
        furnace
(They enjoy the faint warmth, bulging like a dream).
On the wire netting, the droppings of nuclear weapons:
Snow falls on my shoulders, a pigeon sails off alone.

DEATH OF A ZEN POET

Shinkichi Takahashi (1901 - 1987)

It was one of those moments one stands outside one's body, staring at the silhouette, dumbstruck, not wanting to believe words coming in. The phone message from Japan was that the greatest modern Zen poet had died. I waited for the eulogies, a voice to cry out at the passing of a man who made fresh visions of the world, made wild and powerful music out of anything: shells, knitting, peaches, an airplane passing between his legs, the sweet-sour smell coming from a cemetery of unknown soldiers, the crab of memory crawling up a woman's thigh, a sparrow whose stir can move the universe. A man who showed that things loved or despised were, when all's said and done, as important and unimportant as each other. But all was silence as I looked out, hoping for a cloud of his beloved sparrows bearing his karma wheel around the earth.

I realized that he might prefer it this way. Yet there remain the masterworks, his gift to us, in spite of his mixed feelings on the handing down of mere words. "If we sit in Zen at all," he says in the foreword to *Afterimages*, a collection of his poems, "we must model ourselves on the Bodhidharma, who kept sitting till his buttocks grew rotten. We must have done with all words and letters, and attain Truth itself. As a follower of the tradition of Zen which is above verbalization, I must confess that I feel ashamed of writing poems and having collections of them published. My wish is that through books like this the West will awake to the Buddha's Truth. It is my belief that Buddhism will travel round the world till it will bury its old bones in the ridges of the Himalayas."

Yet, paradoxically, Shinkichi Takahashi was one of Japan's most prolific poets, greatly honored (his *Collected Poems* won the Ministry of Education's Prize for Art), thought by the Japanese to be their only poet who could properly be called a Zen poet, for his practice of the discipline was exceptionally pure. He discovered early in life that unless he grappled with the severest of the doctrine's principles he would not be living, or writing, worthily. Yet stuffy as this sounds, there was much humor in him, as in all enlightened Zenists.

AFTERNOON

My hair's falling fast —
this afternoon
I'm off to Asia Minor.

THE PINK SUN

White petals on the black earth,
Their scent filling her nostrils.

Breathe out and all things swell —
Breathe in, they shrink.

Let's suppose she suddenly has four legs —
That's far from fantastic.

I'll weld ox hoofs onto her feet —
Sparks of the camellia's sharp red.

Wagging her pretty little tail,
She's absorbed in kitchen work.

Look, she who just last night
Was a crone is girl again,

An alpine rose blooming on her arm.
High on a Himalayan ridge

The great King of Bhutan
Snores in the pinkest sun.

The poet, born in 1901 in a fishing village on Shikoku, smallest of
Japan's four main islands, was largely self-educated, but broadly so:
writing extensively on many aspects of Japanese culture, he introduced
an important series of art books and had a successful career as a man
of letters. Not bad for one who had dropped out of high school and
rushed off to Tokyo in hope of a literary career. There he contracted
typhus and, penniless, landed in a charity hospital. His cirumstances

163

forced him to return to his village. But one day, fired up by a newspaper article on dadaism, he returned to Tokyo, working as a waiter in a *shiruko* restaurant (*shiruko* is red-bean soup with bits of rice cake) and as a "pantry boy" in a newspaper office, running errands and serving tea.

In 1923 he brought out *Dadaist Shinkichi's Poetry*. The first copy of it was handed him through the bars of a police cell — at this time he was often in trouble for impulsive actions — and he tore it up without so much as a glance. Other collections followed, but by 1928 he knew his life was in dire need of guidance, and like many troubled artists he sought the advice of a Zen master. He could not have chosen better. Shizan Ashikaga, illustrious Rinzai Zen master of the Shogun Temple, was known to be a disciplinarian, one not likely to be impressed by a disciple's literary forays.

At first the toughness of the training proved too much. Pacing the temple corridor, he fell unconscious; when he came to, he was incoherent. Later he was to write that this was inevitable, considering how completely different ascetic exercises were from his daily life and with what youthful single-mindedness he had pursued them. He was sent back to his family and virtually locked up in a small (two-mat) room for three long years. During this confinement he wrote many poems, which may have helped him to survive the ordeal and recover.

Back in Tokyo in 1932, Takahashi began attending Master Shizan Ashikaga's lectures on Zen. Shizan once cautioned him, "Attending lectures cuts no ice. Koan exercise [meditation on Zen problems set by a master] is all-important." Takahashi became his disciple in 1935. During almost seventeen years of rigorous training he experienced both great hardships and exultations of satori. By 1951, having learned all that he could, he was given, in the master's own calligraphy, "The Moon-on-Water Hall" — his *inka*, or testimony that he had successfully completed the full course of discipline, one of only seven over many years so honored by the master.

Takahashi visited Korea and China in 1939 and was deeply impressed by Zenists he met there. He lived chiefly by his writing, and in 1944 began work for a Tokyo newspaper, leaving when its office was bombed out in 1945. He married in 1951 and lived with his wife and their two daughters in great serenity, a life he scarcely could have dreamt of in his turbulent youth.

The poet had distinguished himself in many ways by the time the first translated collection of his poems, *Afterimages*, appeared (simultaneously in the United States and England in 1970) to much acclaim. A reviewer in the *Hudson Review* observed that while other poets, East and West, would appear to descend from time to time into the natural world, Takahashi would emerge from it like a seal from the depths of the sea, his constant element. But it wasn't sea or nature the poet lived in, it was Zen.

Yet that would hardly account for the appeal of his work, especially among fellow poets, throughout the world, with or without interest in Zen. He was foremost an artist. Many aestheticians have spoken of the difficulty of defining art, yet some artists have on occasion chosen to speak out, as did Tolstoy in *What is Art?* Tolstoy identified three essential ingredients of effective art — individuality, clarity, and sincerity — and to the degree that each, in combination with the others, was present, a work could be ranked on a scale of merely acceptable to necessary. Tolstoy was a moralist in all such matters, and never tired of inveighing against aesthetic notions based largely on the pleasure principle, among them "art for art's sake" — life was too serious for such twaddle.

Though as a Zenist Takahashi was not inclined to theorize on literary matters, he might well have agreed with Tolstoy. Surely none would question the sincerity (integrity?) of his work, and that it should be individual, as all true Zen art, is perhaps axiomatic. It is the remaining essential in Tolstoy's triad, clarity, that some may claim is critically missing. But as the poet often said, the very nature of the Zen pursuit, the attainment of spiritual awakening, rules out likelihood of easy accessibility to its arts. "When I write poems," he told me, "no allowances can be made. Thought of a poem's difficulty never troubles me, since I never consciously make poems difficult."

A major reason for the difficulty of Zen poems, throughout the fifteen hundred years they have been written, is that many, perhaps the best known and most valued in and out of Zen communities, are those of "mutual understanding" (*agyo* or *toki-no-ge* in Japanese). Such poems are basically koan interpretations, as is the following piece, "Collapse," written by Takahashi early in Zen training:

> Time oozed from my pores,
> Drinking tea
> I tasted the seven seas.
>
> I saw in the mist formed
> Around me
> The fatal chrysanthemum, myself.

Its scent choked, and as I
Rose, squaring
My shoulders, the earth collapsed.

This, Takahashi told me, was written in response to a koan his master asked him to meditate on, one often given disciples early in training, "Describe your face before you were begotten by your parents." We observe the poet deep in *zazen* (formal Zen meditation), experiencing the extraordinary expansions and penetrations sometimes realized by the meditator. Suddenly, in the mist, he sees that face and is repulsed ("Its scent choked"). He rises, freed from it, ready for anything. The old world breaks up, and he enters the new.

Though Takahashi was always forthcoming with me about circumstances that may have led to the making of such poems (I was, after all, his translator), he was reluctant to reveal the manner in which they were received by the master, feeling such revelations would be too intimate. That attitude is only natural, perhaps, and besides, Zenists are cautioned to avoid such disclosures. The poet did confide, however, that the following was his versification of the master's response to one of his koan-based poems:

WORDS

I don't take your words
Merely as words.
Far from it.

I listen
To what makes you talk —
Whatever that is —
And me listen.

It is intriguing to imagine the scene: poet sitting before master for *sanzen* (a meeting for discussion of progress with koan), daring to complain that his interpretive poem was being misunderstood. "Words," expressing more than gentle reproach, relates intimately to a special bond, while at the same time it defines perhaps the nature of such talk, in or out of a *zendo* (meditation hall). As one might suppose, there are no correct interpretations. The koan is meant to dislodge, throw off

166

balance, and the adequate poem reveals to what degree the disciple has righted himself — nothing more or less. And the more successful the interpretation, the finer the poem as poem.

The poem of mutual understanding, important to Zen since the T'ang dynasty, is a clear gauge of progress in discipline. It is not "poem" until such judgment is made, not by a literary critic but by a qualified master. Most awakening poems are of this type, though hardly planned or anticipated. Only a master, aware of his disciple's needs, lacks and strengths, knows whether the longed-for breakthrough has been made. The poem tells all, accompanied of course by numerous signs in conduct itself, in speech, walk, work and relationships with others.

The Japanese master Daito (1282-1337), when a disciple, was given by his master the eighth koan of *Hekiganroku*, a Chinese work of great antiquity made up of one hundred Zen problems with commentary. Daito, who gained satori from his struggle with the koan, wrote at least two poems of mutual understanding based on it. Here is the text of the koan and the two most important poems it inspired:

Attention! Suigan, at the end of the summer, spoke to the assembly and said: "For the whole summer I have lectured to the brethren. Look! Has Suigan any eyebrows?" Hofuko said, "He who does robberies has a heart of deceit." Chokei said, "They grow." Unmon said, "A barrier!"

> Unmon's barrier pulled down, the old
> Path lost. Blue sky's my home,
> My every action beyond man's reach:
> A golden priest, arms folded, has returned.
>
> At last I've broken Unmon's barrier!
> There's exit everywhere — east, west; north, south.
> In at morning, out at evening; neither host nor guest.
> My every step stirs up a little breeze.

Not all awakening poems are written in response to koan. Often a master, in normal conversation, will unconsciously challenge disciples to grapple with more general things. The subject of Time is much discussed in Zen communities. Takahashi once told me that the following lines came about that way.

TIME

Time like a lake breeze
Touched his face.
All thought left his mind.

One morning the sun, menacing,
Rose from behind a mountain,
Singeing — like hope — the trees.

Fully awakened, he lit his pipe
And assumed the sun-inhaling pose:
Time poured down — like rain, like fruit.

He glanced back and saw a ship
Moving toward the past. In one hand
He gripped the sail of eternity,

And stuffed the universe into his eyes.

The American poet Richard Ronan, in his master's thesis, "Process and Mastery in Bashō and Wallace Stevens," dealt most convincingly with this and other Takahashi poems. He wrote:

'The "lake breeze" is an allusion to the Hindu concept of *nirvana*, literally to be "blown away," a concept from which the Japanese satori, enlightenment, is derived. Reaching *nirvana/satori*, one's relativity is necessarily blown away, leaving only one's essential nature, which is identical to that of the Void, the Buddhist Absolute. Having conquered the sun of Time, the speaker inhales it, absurdly smoking his pipe. He consumes the universe by seeing it for the first time as it is. "Devouring time" is devoured by the poet's *satori* conquest of the relative.'

The conquest of the relative, the leap from the conditioned to an unconditioned plateau of being, is the extraordinary goal of Zen, and it is the reigning paradox of Zen art that work so private, of "mutual understanding," should have such broad appeal. In order for the Zenist to take the leap, he must attain a state of no-mind (*wu-hsin* in Chinese) — "All thought left his mind" in Takahshi's "Time" — an essential precondition of *muga*, the full identification of observer and observed.

The aesthetic term *zenkan* (pure seeing) has application to all Zen arts, and what it implies about the practitioner is startling: somehow he has won through, crushed the hungering ego, which in the unenlightened bars realization. The true Zen artist, of whatever medium, is a man risen from that smoldering.

Among modern poets, East and West, Shinkichi Takahashi was distinguished largely through the practice of *zenkan*, identifying effortlessly with all he observed, through which he ennobled not only his art but life itself. Like all awakened Zenists he found no separation between art and life, knowing the achievement of no-mind led not only to right art but to right living. He rarely used such general terms, but on occasion would explain what that practice of *zenkan* had meant to him. As an artist, he had engaged for years in intense, unobstructed observation. Things moving, stationary; one no more appropriate than another, no circumstance more or less favorable. He always cautioned, as he himself had been, against dualism, assuring that little by little one learns to know true seeing from false, that it was possible to reach the unconditioned. The world, he claimed, is always pure — we, with our dripping mind-stuff, foul it.

So puzzling to most of us. In the West some — Paul Valery for one — without reference to Zen or other disciplines, turned in horror from the shifting mind, all a-wobble, twisted this way and that, filled with anxieties. Such men have spoken out of the need to subdue the mind, crush the ego, but where have they offered the way to make that possible? We don't appreciate how wise we are when we speak of troubles being "only in the mind," for born and heavily nourished there, they become giants that slay. When emptied of them and pointed properly, the mind is no longer a destructive agent: it is the only light we need. Zen has been saying this for fifteen hundred years, never more effectively than through its poets, among whom in our lifetime Shinkichi Takahashi was the most profound.

I last saw the poet in the summer of 1985. He had insisted on postponing entering the hospital so that we might meet at his home in Tokyo. Ten years had passed since our last meeting, in the very same room. Though much changed, so weak he could not stand, there was the same vitality in his voice, the old sparkle in his eyes. In the past we had met chiefly to discuss his poems, pieces I was attempting with Takashi Ikemoto's help to render into English. Now we laughed together with his gentle wife, remembering old moments. When a common friend took out a camera, he begged him not to waste the film on him but to instead photograph his *inka* framed on the wall. Suddenly he looked up, smiled at me and said, "You have seen me on the path of life. Now I am on the path of death." As he spoke, lines from his poem "Life Infinite" flashed through my mind:

> Beyond words, this no-thingness within,
> Which I've become. So to remain
>
> Only one thing's needed: Zen sitting.
> I think, breathe with my whole body —
>
> Marvellous. The joy's so pure,
> It's beyond lovemaking, anything.
>
> I can see, live anywhere, everywhere.
> I need nothing, not even life.

Shinkichi Takahashi was a remarkable poet. Few in our time have encompassed so much, left such a bracing legacy. How he achieved so much will, I am confident, engage the minds and talents of future scholars, but this I will claim for him: he found early in life what his life most needed, lived it, and wrote it as no other could.

The poet died the night of June 4, 1987. I could only lift my head with gratitude for having known him, and now offer to his memory a few words:

June 5, 1987

While I wash dishes to
Gregorian chants, what
started out a ho-hum
day — the usual round

of doodles, chores,
anxieties — explodes
with a bright swallowtail
joyriding by the window,

looping where by whitest
columbines a robin, head
cocked to love sounds,
watches as a squirrel

near the old pear tree
quivers astride his mate.
The phone rings, bringing
word Shinkichi Takahashi

died last night.
    And so
the world goes on. Now
the squirrels scamper

through the branches,
making leaves dance
like the poet's sparrows
wing-stroking an elegy in air.

LUCIEN STRYK

AFTERWORD

Poetry and Lentil Soup
A PROFILE OF LUCIEN STRYK

Susan Porterfield

I'm eating lunch with Lucien Stryk at his home in DeKalb, Illinois. He has returned from London for a few weeks to keep reading tour engagements in the East and while here to be interviewed by me. His wife of more than forty years, Helen, has remained abroad.

Instead of one of her renowned meals, I'm eating canned lentil soup into which Stryk has tossed mushrooms, likewise canned, and sliced, red onions. On the side we have tinned salmon mixed with the remainder of the onion, which has been marinated with apple cider vinegar, a consort of grapes and bananas drizzled with blueberry syrup, and toasted bagels.

It's surprisingly good.

In fact, Stryk seems to have a way of finding what will work in almost any situation, domestic or otherwise, compelling hidden unities to reveal themselves amid apparent differences. This is so, I suspect, because for him the world isn't fragmented, fractured, or blasted. Men and women may be, in their responses to it. But the world itself is perfect.

The disparity may explain something about why he writes: to move beyond his partial, ego-centered perception toward the genuine; to come as close to it as he can; to approach via the word.

Stryk belongs to a tradition that considers the true artist to be a hero, a visionary, a prophet, someone to whom others may turn. The natural artist can see or at the very least, tries to see what others don't, and he or she is capable of creating a thing of beauty. Because poetry is frighteningly important, the nature of those who write it is just as significant. "We write what we are," he tells me, then interrupts himself, pointing to a cardinal in the fir tree behind me outside. "And what we are matters."

Who is Lucien Stryk? His life unfolds narratively, event leading to event, leading to epiphanic moment, and its story-like quality is part of its romance, part of its appeal. Most simply, he's a good Midwestern son, a boy from the heartland, reared in Chicago.

His father, Emil, a paint-store-owning sculptor, knew many of the artists and writers of Chicago, among them Ben Hecht and Maxwell Bodenheim. Emil Stryk took his son to the Art Institute, to the studios of the Kemp brothers, one a painter and the other a wood carver; he prompted the boy to memorize poems, and later when Stryk was older, encouraged him to read the family's subscription to *Les Temps Modernes*, the periodical begun by Jean-Paul Sartre in 1945. Growing up in an environment supportive of the arts, Stryk was naturally drawn to them. "Quite early I felt I might work as a writer, although I didn't know in what direction. I knew that in important art, I could find something for myself."

His Chicago upbringing aside, Stryk is also a native European, born in Poland and brought to the country by way of Ellis Island in the late 1920's when he was about four years old. We discuss how this experience is, paradoxically perhaps, typically an American one, how the dual cultural identity of many of his generation of artists has contributed to our current artistic heritage, particularly regarding the widespread interest in translation.

"The American is famously exploratory: we've engaged with other cultures since childhood. I remember Italians, Greeks in my old neighborhood. From our earliest years we're exposed to different cultures." The result may be that we are more accustomed to hearing the voices of those different from ourselves. Stryk finds this "migration of cultures across boundaries through the vehicle of poetry" one of the most positive characteristics of American letters.

Certainly his numerous experiences abroad have contributed to the formation of his own poetry. During World War II, for example, he served on Okinawa and Saipan as a forward observer, scouting the position of enemy troops. This ordeal and other trials of war eventually proved crucial to his art as did his days spent at the Sorbonne. Stryk came home to Chicago from the War in late 1945 but three years later left the States again, this time to live the life of the student-intellectual in the heady atmosphere of post-war Paris. Here, studying under Gaston Bachelard, Stryk read philosophy, frequented the Cafe Mabillon where he often met his friend, Jean-Paul Baudot, the young Resistance fighter of Stryk's poem "Letter to Jean-Paul Baudot, at Christmas," nightwalked along the banks of the Seine, fell in and out of love, and dreamed.

Paris *is* a movable feast and proved to be so for Stryk, who remained there for two years from 1948-1950. Important things were happening for him. He began to know how he might live in the arts, in what direction he would go. Up in his tiny left-bank lodging at the Hôtel de Buci, he began seriously to write poetry. His poem "Rooms" tells how he'd "Read through the dictionary, stalking/new words for verse . . ."

in the g's, for granadilla —

where visions of stigmata, nail marks,
thorns became a poem heavy with
may-pops, fruit of the passionflower.

(Bells of Lombardy,
Northern Illinois University Press, 1986)

After Paris, Stryk went to England to study at the University of London. There he met his wife, an Englishwoman who worked in a local bookstore and who noticed the young, serious-minded American flipping through journals that contained his work, too poor to buy copies. In the 1950's, Stryk's first two books of poetry appeared, *Taproot* (1953) and *Trespasser* (1956) both published by the British house, Fantasy Press. He also became a father.

But he wasn't quite ready to settle down. In 1961-62, with the Shah of Iran in power, Stryk held a Fulbright lectureship in Meshed. He and his wife tell tales about learning to censor themselves concerning the activities of some of his students who otherwise might suddenly disappear. Stryk also circled the globe twice, once on a tramp steamer, and happily recalls the exotic ports, the people, the free-flowing wine.

Despite these adventures, no place has affected him as profoundly as Japan. While stationed on the mainland during the autumn of 1945, shortly before he was discharged, he promised himself that one day he'd return to learn about this country. Through the course of two subsequent visits there, the first lasting from 1956 through 1958 and the second from 1962 to 1963, he discovered something that would change his life.

He learned how to write poetry. "Above and beyond the desire to make oneself an artist," he realized then and still very much believes, "one must make oneself a more complete human being." Until this point, despite receiving an MFA from the University of Iowa in 1956, and having published two books of poetry with Fantasy Press, he hadn't yet found his voice.

But after two Zenists admonished him for asking naive questions about Buddhism, Stryk says in the essay "Making Poems" from his book *Encounter with Zen* (Ohio University Press/Swallow, 1981), he became determined to understand. What he learned changed his life and led him to revise completely pieces that he'd once considered finished. He began writing poetry different from anything he'd previously done. At one crucial point, he stayed up all night working on "Zen: The Rocks of Sesshu," which was his initial attempt in verse to come to terms with first principles. "To be an artist," he says, "you must become a larger human being, more compassionate, more concerned, more aware." Not surprisingly, the next book, *Notes for a Guidebook* (Ohio University Press/Swallow, 1965), which he considers his first real book of poetry, would not appear for nine more long, contemplative, patient years.

Even now, after publishing more than thirty books of his own poetry, translations of Zen works, and editions of collected poetry, Stryk continues to learn about himself as poet and about the art he loves. On the first day of our interview, he was kind enough to show me revisions of some poems that I'd heard him read several months before. "I love discovering I've been an ass and then returning to the work and making something of it, discovering that I've been given another chance."

He is sitting in his recliner, feet up, relaxed. For a man of seventy, Stryk radiates the energy of a person half his age. He has, in fact, just driven from Virginia to his home in Illinois in one day. "It is very easy for a practicing poet to delude himself simply by looking at something and coming up with effective detailing and, *voila* — a poem," he tells me. "But the poetry has not been found. One has lied to oneself." This delusion, he says, produces art that is immoral.

Zen teachings insist that the character of the artist determines the quality of his or her work. Because Stryk finds this idea to be crucial to both art and life, he continues to study and translate Zen texts. Many of the poems are traditionally written in response to *koan* (Zen riddles or paradoxical problems for meditation) set by a master, who judges them not for their own aesthetic sakes but as evidence of his disciple's spiritual condition. The most accomplished poems come only to the enlightened few.

Because Zen poetry can reveal the enlightened thought of its authors, translators of it, according to Stryk, must try to achieve an analogous spiritual level or else risk producing inferior work. "Some may see the translator's attempt as arrogant," Stryk admits, "but even if his worthiness lasts only for the moment, it must be so."

"Who owns the text then," I ask him, thinking the question a tough one, "the poet or the translator?"

"The translator," he says without a quiver, and adds that this is true regardless of the kind of poem, whether Zen or not. His own poetry, for example, has been rendered into Swedish, Italian, French, and Russian. These versions of his work, he feels, belong to their foreign authors. To be a good translator, you must "live the poems, breathe them," he tells me; you must identify yourself with the poet, regardless of the century, gender, or culture.

I ask to see Stryk's study, and he leads me to a small room in the rear of the house where we continue the interview. One wall of windows is half covered on the outside with bushes, home to tiny birds that live in the intricacies of the branches. His desk is semi-circular and smallish. The typewriter, which he only uses at a certain, advanced stage in the composing process, rests on a table to the left. He distrusts computers, feeling their capacity for generating tidy text can deceive writers into thinking they've completed their work.

On the wall next to his desk hangs a scroll painted by the eighteenth-century artist, Taiga. It is one of his most prized possessions. "Sometimes, at dawn," for he's an early riser, "the sun comes in these windows and falls on the scroll in such a way, ... Can you imagine this? I practically do a little dance for joy, just to see it." That same joy, or energy, or whatever it is, led him to circle the globe, to search for and find "the art to make life possible" in a world whose myths the War had exploded.

Stryk is never anything but excited about life, whether he is listening to a favorite aria, walking in the park, which he does every morning, rain or shine, admiring his favorite Guardi or Goya paintings at the Art Institute in Chicago, or even eating canned lentil soup. "We look in art for passionate engagements with the things of this world. And passionate commitment to ideals. There can't be good art without passion."

"Is the person in the act of writing a poem different from the same person not writing, when he or she takes out the garbage, for example, or balances the checkbook?" I ask.

And again, he doesn't hesitate. "We are never free of the obligation to respond to the world. The poet, if he's any good, is always a poet. To the eyes of others, he may be considerably different, but it could very well be that the poet's struggle with a poem may occur anywhere, in class teaching, driving somewhere. The poet doesn't keep office hours."

176

Stryk happens to do much of his writing in the morning, but he says he likes knowing that a poem could come at anytime, anywhere, be about anything. "What we want is discovery, and I think the finest discoveries are made when one is not looking. Such discoveries are often small, an observation, something seen freshly. Then suddenly, because of the poet's state of mind at the time he perceives this thing, that perception crystallizes, and hence in the most organic way a poem begins." While some poets claim they often know nothing else about a poem except how it will end, Stryk says just the opposite. "Every poem turns out differently from what I expected, makes its shifts, goes through its disguises, waits for me to rip off its disguises."

Through his translations of important haiku, Stryk has developed such a high regard for the art that he feels unqualified to achieve anything worthy enough of his own in the form. He does favor a construct that is haiku-like, however, tercets, sometimes couplets, composed of short lines. He finds that the way the first lines arrange themselves, "stretch, fall across the page, the tonal resonance," is extremely important for the poem as a whole. "It has to do with the way we breathe, the way our eyes take in detail."

He gives me an example: "Two poets look out the window at the same scene with the thought of describing it. Working in the way most natural to them, one will need twenty words and the other seventy-five. The one needing only twenty is likely to choose the couplet or tercet; the other will need something ampler. Now if you were to ask, they'd say 'Why, purely aesthetic reasons' determine their choices. The eye fills the space with what it requires. A choice has been made, a limitation accepted."

As he speaks, I happen to notice that the curtains on the windows of his study are fastened open with neckties. I pause in my questioning to bring this fact casually to his attention. He confesses and admits to disliking watches as well. We agree that there are certain limitations one cannot accept.

Still, Stryk has turned most of his into blessings that structure the narrative of his life. There is something appealing about someone who has found a way that endures. He continues to learn about and write poetry and has brought out two new books in 1995. Both *The Awakened Self: Encounters with Zen* (Kodansha America) and *Zen Poetry: Let the Spring Breeze Enter* (Grove/Atlantic) contain his translations of Zen poetry.

He remains certain as well that there is such a thing as a poetic disposition. "Otherwise," he says, "there'd be no point." If, in other words, poetry does anything more than entertain, if it can provide answers, guide us, teach us, inspire us, then who the poet is becomes important. For Stryk, poetry depends upon the sensibility of the artist, upon a "generosity of spirit, an openness that leads the poet to embrace many things that on the surface might seem unpromising." The more an artist looks beyond the self, "to a keen awareness of the human journey, the more likely he is to win through, to achieve something important."

"Could an immoral person be a poet?" I ask.

"I can't imagine an immoral person bothering with poetry," he shoots back, "and by 'immoral,' I'm not talking about trivialities. I mean in the largest sense, in the way a person relates to the world, his spirit. In the poets that affect me, there is always that element of desire and hope."

> I thirsted seasons,
> dragging a leaden shadow
> into nothingness. Now,
>
> as fire meets ice, I see.

("*Lake Dawn*" from "*The City: A Cycle*," *Collected Poems*, Ohio University Press/ Swallow, 1984.)

SKOOB *Pacifica*

Contemporary writings of the Pacific Rim and South Asia

Skoob Pacifica is a new series which brings to a wider reading public the best in contemporary fiction, poetry, drama and criticism from the countries of the Pacific Rim. The flagship of the series, the Skoob Pacifica Anthology, presents selections from many of our featured authors alongside those of more established names.

SKOOB PACIFICA ANTHOLOGY No.1
S.E.Asia Writes Back!
I.K.Ong & C.Y.Loh (editors)

An eclectic blend of prose, poetry, drama and reportage which creates a vibrant picture of the post-colonial world. Featured writers include Vikram Seth, Yukio Mishima and Wole Soyinka, with short stories by Yasunari Kawabata and Derek Walcott.
ISBN 1 871438 19 5   432pp   £5.99 $10.95

SKOOB PACIFICA ANTHOLOGY No.2
The Pen is Mightier Than The Sword

This second anthology focuses on exciting and challenging writing from Malaysia and Singapore in the 1990s. Also featured are pieces by Han Suyin, Toni Morrison and V.S. Naipaul.
ISBN 1 871438 54 3   412pp   £6.99 $11.99

SKOOB PACIFICA ANTHOLOGY No.3
Exiled in Paradise

In this third volume, the scope of the series is extended to include South Asia, an important area of new writing. It also contains poetry from the Philippines, and includes work from Naguib Mahfouz, Nadine Gordimer and Shirley Geok-lin Lim.
ISBN 1 871438 59 4   432pp   £6.99   Forthcoming